GREEK MYTHS

GREEK MYTHS

MARTIN J. DOUGHERTY

First published in 2019

Copyright © 2019 Amber Books Ltd

All rights reserved. No part of this publication may be reproduced, stored in a retrieval system, or transmitted in any form or by any means, electronic, mechanical, photocopying, recording, or otherwise, without prior written permission of the copyright holder.

Published by
Amber Books Ltd
United House
North Road
London
N7 9DP
United Kingdom
www.amberbooks.co.uk
Instagram: amberbooksltd
Facebook: www.facebook.com/amberbooks
Twitter: @amberbooks

ISBN: 978-1-78274-750-5

Project Editor: Sarah Uttridge
Designer: Hart McLeod Ltd.
Picture Research: Terry Forshaw

Printed in China

CONTENTS

Introduction		6
Chapter 1	Cosmology and Creation	22
Chapter 2	The Olympian Gods	52
Chapter 3	Other Gods and Spirits	92
Chapter 4	The World of Gods and Mortals	126
Chapter 5	Heroes and War	156
Chapter 6	The Legacy of Greek Mythology	198
Bibliography		218
Index		219

INTRODUCTION

Greece was the birthplace of one of the greatest civilizations the world has ever seen; one that influenced its contemporaries and laid the foundations for others that came after. Its scholars were pioneers of science, mathematics, medicine and philosophy.

Its architects created a style that is still influential today. Greek traders brought civilization and new ideas to the lands of those they called 'barbarians', and Greek warriors fought in the great wars of their era. The legends of this great civilization are still recounted today.

The history of Ancient Greece is as complex as its mythology, and indeed there are parallels to the rise of Greek civilization within the tales of their gods and heroes. Some legends have at times been believed as fact, then later dismissed as invention, only for evidence to surface that they may indeed have been based on real events.

OPPOSITE: Even those with no interest in mythology can identify at least some of the gods of Olympus. Recognizable depictions of Zeus, Poseidon, Pan and many others have become part what might be called 'modern popular mythology'.

Greek mythology is pervasive within Western culture. Warships, space missions and clothing brands all carry names from legend. The Apollo moon missions were named for a Greek god of wisdom and light; the Aegis missile defence system takes its name from a shield associated with Zeus and Athena. Giving a mythological title to an important project implies a suitable level of grandeur and magnificence. It can also increase sales of more mundane items.

Today, the gods, heroes and monsters of Greek legend form part of what might be called a 'popular mythology' that is familiar worldwide. If a supernatural-themed movie or television show contains a reference to ancient Greek gods or heroes, there is no need to explain them to the audience. Most viewers will already know, in general terms at least, who or what they are hearing about.

What we know about the complex mythology of Ancient Greece comes partly from historians and poets writing much later, and partly from evidence preserved in art and architecture. It is likely that the version of Greek mythology generally accepted in modern times is not wholly accurate – Ancient Greece had a long history and its myths will have developed over time.

The roles and capabilities of the gods and monsters will have changed and evolved, and some previously important figures may have been diminished or even forgotten entirely. However, there is enough evidence, from a sufficiently wide range of sources, to form a picture of ancient Greek mythology that can be considered broadly accurate. More than that may be impossible to achieve; such is the nature of mythology.

Origins of the Greek Peoples

It has long been accepted that humans evolved in Africa and spread to other regions, although exactly when and how remains a subject for debate. Recent discoveries have caused some scientists to challenge the traditional theory of African origin, suggesting that the earliest ancestors of humans may have developed in southern Europe.

BELOW: Clay vessels and cave art found on Crete prove that humans were present in the islands of the Mediterranean during the Neolithic era, which began around 12,000 years ago.

ABOVE: A hunting scene carved on Naxos island. It is possible that images such as this were believed to bring good luck in the hunt, and are thus evidence of religion or spiritual beliefs.

There is only a small amount of evidence for this, however, and the theory is not widely accepted.

Be that as it may, there are indications that human ancestors were present in Greece several million years ago, long before the first migrations of ancestral humans are thought to have taken place. This does not necessarily contradict accepted theories; sea levels have changed considerably due to a series of ice ages, and migration of small numbers of humans by way of islands and land bridges is not impossible.

The same series of ice ages has destroyed much of the evidence of habitation in Europe. Evidence has been found of ancestral humans in various parts of Europe before the Last Glacial Maximum, which occurred 20–25,000 years ago, but it is likely that glaciation drove humans completely out of Europe. By the time the ice retreated, behaviourally modern humans had appeared, and it was these people who repopulated the lands left behind by the melting ice sheets.

It is not clear exactly when humans spread into what is now Greece and the surrounding islands. Cave art has been found on the island of Crete dating from at least 11,000 years ago, a time when the climate was generally warming after the end of the last ice age. It is possible that humans inhabited the area before that, but thus far no clear evidence has been found.

These people were Palaeolithic (early Stone Age) hunter-gatherers, living in small bands and working with stone tools. They were anatomically and behaviourally like modern humans, who engaged in ritual behaviour and were capable of abstract thought. We do not know what stories they told of how the world came to be or the deeds of their gods, but they would have asked the same questions as anyone else: How did we come to be here? How does the world work? What is over the next hill? and What will happen if I…?

The questions these early people asked led to experimentation and progress. Around 7000BC, the Neolithic era (new, or late, Stone Age) began in what is now Greece. There was no sharp cut-off point or moment of change, but a gradual advancement in technology took place. More sophisticated stone tools were introduced, and crafts began to develop such as weaving and the making of pottery.

Each of these new developments meant that the people of prehistoric Greece could do something a little better or take less time to complete a task, improving their chances of survival and making further progress. They lived in small communities of perhaps 50–100 people, herding animals and farming the land. As the climate stabilized after the end of the ice age, populations expanded and groups pushed into new areas to claim them.

The Neolithic people of Greece had both the time and the desire to decorate their pottery, suggesting that they preferred finer things to mere utilitarian tools. They took the time to decorate pottery because the end result was pleasing, and perhaps because a finely made item could be traded to a

BELOW: The decoration on this bronze helmet, dating from around 1600–1450BC, indicates that while conflict was common, society was stable and prosperous enough to create quality items whose value went beyond their functionality.

prosperous neighbour. This kind of activity is only possible in a successful, thriving society where life is more than a battle for survival, which in turn implies that these ancient people were skilled and capable of overcoming a variety of problems to maintain their lifestyle.

The Helladic Era

By around 3000BC, the people of ancient Greece had learned to work metal. At first this was copper, ushering in the short Chalcolithic or Copper Age. Copper can be found in its native state, and both extracted and worked without the need for extreme heating. The results are usually rather crude, however, and the characteristics that made copper accessible also meant it was a poor tool-making metal. The invention of bronze allowed the creation of durable tools, finally making stone obsolete for most purposes.

ABOVE: Kraters, or 'mixing vessels', were common in Greek society. Large and heavy when filled with watered wine, they were placed in the centre of a room at a gathering. Smaller drinking vessels were then filled from the krater.

The adoption of bronze-working was not instantaneous. The need to assemble copper, tin and other minerals at a suitable place for metal-working, and the time required to produce items of good quality, meant that bronze was expensive. Much of the metal-working of the period was concerned with decorative items such as jewellery made of gold, silver and copper rather than tools and weapons.

This period is known as the Helladic era, and during it metal-working and other crafts spread among the villages of ancient Greece. Rising populations and larger settlements made it possible for specialist craftspeople to emerge as a social class. Social stratification became more pronounced over time, enabling the emergence of kingdoms with an elite ruling and warrior class.

Rise of the Minoan Civilization

Modern scholars subdivide the Helladic era into phases, characterized by pottery styles. This is largely due to the availability of evidence; pottery tends to survive, at least in the form of fragments, whereas fabrics decay, tools are worn out and structures are built over. Social and technological development was not uniform, and there were periods of regression in some areas while the communities in others continued to mature.

The greatest civilization of the Helladic era was the Minoan culture, although its inhabitants would not have used that name for themselves; it is a modern application derived from the legend of King Minos and his labyrinth. The Minoan culture was based around palaces that apparently served as religious and trade centres. These first appeared around 2000BC, and appear to have been rebuilt three centuries later after destruction by earthquakes and other disasters. They do not appear to have been fortified, although weaponry and war gear have been found in archaeological digs, suggesting that the Minoan civilization was largely, if not entirely, peaceful.

The Minoan civilization developed on Crete and spread to the surrounding islands, trading with Egypt and lands all

BELOW: **Bull-leaping, often in connection with bull-worship, was practiced in several contemporary civilizations but is primarily associated with the Minoan culture. Merely evading the bull's charge was not enough; the brave participant was expected to perform acrobatic feats.**

around the eastern end of the Mediterranean. In its heyday, the Minoan culture produced great works of art, including frescoes that have survived into modern times. Some of these depict sports such as bull-leaping, which appears to have been very popular, tying in with the legend of a bull-headed minotaur dwelling in Minos's labyrinth.

Minoan civilization began to decline around 1500BC, for reasons that remain unclear. It is possible that a combination of natural disasters such as earthquakes or volcanic eruptions and the rise of other powers in the region undermined the power of the Minoans and rendered them vulnerable to invasion, or they may have fallen victim to internal divisions. By around 1200BC, the Minoan civilization had ceased to exist.

One factor in the fall of the Minoan civilization may have been the rise of the Mycenaean culture in mainland Greece. Mycenaean civilization was certainly influenced by the Minoan culture, and may have been founded as an offshoot of it. The Mycenaean people were more warlike than the Minoans, possibly as a result of land links to aggressive neighbours.

The Mycenaeans, like the Minoans, built labyrinthine palace complexes, but these were fortified with walls of large stone blocks. Mycenaean stone-working was rather basic, generally using undressed stone for projects such as fortifications and dams. However, their palaces and towns were decorated with frescoes and sculptures that show Minoan influences but also the emergence of a distinct Mycenaean style.

In addition to Mycenae itself, the Mycenaean civilization included a number of regions that would be important in later Greek history: Athens, Argos, Sparta and Thebes, among others. Mycenaean merchants engaged in maritime trade around the

ABOVE: **Cup-bearers were more than mere servants. They had direct access to a ruler or other important figure as they served his drinks, and were often party to secrets or involved in intrigues within the court.**

eastern end of the Mediterranean, reaching as far afield as Sicily and probably operating vessels on the Black Sea. Mycenaean goods were traded in Egypt and the cities of Mesopotamia.

The Mycenaean civilization came to an end around 1200BC, during the Bronze Age Collapse that brought down several states around the eastern Mediterranean. The exact causes of this disintegration of civilization are unclear, although climate change may have played a part. Coastal areas were raided and cities sacked by what are referred to in contemporary sources as 'the Sea Peoples'.

The Sea Peoples may or may not have been a single group. It is not known whether they were a culture, a state or perhaps an alliance of pirates. They were certainly powerful, however; over a period of a few years, the coastal cities of the eastern Mediterranean were attacked and pillaged, one after another, leaving behind only ruins in many cases. Egypt built what may have been the world's first organized navy to defend its northern shore, but other civilizations collapsed.

At the same time, a fresh wave of migrant people, the Dorians, was entering Greece from the east. They were by no means the first, but their arrival resulted in enormous upheaval and the displacement of other ethnic groups. The Achaeans, who had dominated the Peloponnese, were overrun and absorbed, or else fled to Cyprus. The other two major ethnic groups of ancient Greece, the Ionians and the Aeolians, were pushed east. They eventually settled on the coasts and islands of the Aegean Sea.

The Greek Dark Age

The Dorian incursion may have been the origin of the Sea Peoples, either directly or as a result of secondary displacement. It ultimately led to the ethnic and cultural distribution of the Greek people when civilization re-emerged, but in the meantime a 'dark age' descended, lasting from around 1200BC to 800BC.

During this period, major urban centres were partially or wholly abandoned. The population dropped sharply, perhaps due to plagues or disrupted food production, and there are signs of technological regression. The common definition of a 'dark age' is a lack of written records, and this was certainly the case in ancient Greece. Most of what is known about the period comes from archaeological research or inferences made from the records of other cultures.

It does appear that conflict occurred during the Greek Dark Age, and that maritime raiding was not uncommon. Society had previously been subject to a fairly uniform set of influences dating back to Minos and Mycenae, but the more fragmented population of the Greek Dark Age began to develop regional variations. Pottery styles diverged, as did burial practices and presumably the rituals that went with them.

Eventually, the old urban sites were repopulated and a new Greek culture began to emerge, one of city-states rather than unified states. The world had changed during the Greek Dark Age, and technology had advanced. Iron-working had begun to become prevalent in the interim, although bronze was still in widespread use, and new cultures had arisen along the borders of what would become Greece.

BELOW: The ancient kings of Athens were largely mythical individuals. The last of them, Codrus, disguised himself as a peasant and picked a fight with some Dorian soldiers, thereby derailing a prophecy that Athens would fall if her king remained unharmed.

The Archaic Period

Literacy re-emerged in ancient Greece after the end of the Dark Age, although written records of the period 800–700BC are scarce. However, the new states of Greece grew rapidly and developed fresh ideas of government and law. Many of the Greek city-states were ruled by 'tyrants', although the term did not have such negative connotations as it does today. A tyrant was an absolute ruler, and therefore capable of doing great ill if they so chose, but many were wise and moderate.

No formal body of law was available at the beginning of the Archaic period, and disputes were generally settled with violence or the threat of it. Feuds could run for many years and draw in outsiders, disrupting society and economic activity. Efforts to curb this disruption began with the issue of rulings by the aristocracy of the

LEFT: **At the end of the Greek Dark Age, around 800BC, artistic styles had changed as this clay doll shows.**

Ancient laws

The earliest known code of laws in Ancient Greece was created by Draco, in around 620BC. The harshness of these laws is itself a legend – Draco and his code of laws gave us the word 'draconian'. The death penalty was applied for even quite minor infractions, and Draco himself insisted that it was merited. However, within a few years, a more moderate version was put in place, which had the effect of protecting the poor and landless from the whims of the aristocracy – to some extent, at least.

Legal developments were accompanied by social changes, reducing the amount of feuding and lawlessness in the cities. Greater stability permitted the development of an extensive trade network, and in time this resulted in the establishment of colonies. Some of these would eventually grow into major societies in their own right. In the meantime, they were instrumental in spreading Greek culture throughout the Mediterranean.

RIGHT: **Draco's code was introduced in 621BC.**

ABOVE: At the Battle of Salamis in 480BC, a Greek fleet defeated the greatly superior Persian navy. This in turn made it difficult for Persia to support its land forces in Greece, and paved the way for a final Greek victory on land.

city, although self-interest and corruption made this a less than attractive prospect for those without the money or power to secure a favourable outcome.

The Archaic period was characterized by wars with Persia, during which Greece faced invasion on several occasions. Famous battles of the era, at Salamis, Thermopylae and Marathon, among others, have become legendary in modern times, and the final repulse of Persia represents the transition from the Archaic to the Classical era.

The Classical Era

The Classical period, or Golden Age began around 480BC, with the end of the Persian wars. Conflict and rivalry between Greek city-states arose partly out of the defeat of Persia at the Battle of Salamis, which ended the prospect of invasion for the foreseeable future. The major city-states vied for supremacy in Greece and the wider Mediterranean world, using politics, economic warfare and outright conflict to further their interests and retain control of distant colonies.

The Peloponnesian War of 431–404BC pitted Athens and what amounted to its maritime empire against the land-based military power of Sparta. Like all Greek conflicts, this was not a simple matter, with other city-states becoming involved or taking advantage of a developing situation to further their own ends. Although the power of Athens was greatly reduced, its cultural influence remained strong.

During this period, great works, such as the Parthenon at Athens, were undertaken that still stand today. The concept of democracy was also established, although its form was different from modern concepts of democratic rule. Membership of the primary decision-making body, the assembly, was open to all males over 18, and many important roles in society such as jurors and magistrates were held on a short-term basis. These were assigned by lot rather than election, which reduced the possibility of institutionalized corruption even if it did not guarantee suitability. Decisions were taken by the assembly on the basis of a majority vote, even on complex matters such as treaties and trade agreements.

This reliance on short-term non-experts and mass decisions could lead to short-sighted decisions, but this was counterbalanced to some extent by the duty of all citizens to understand politics and affairs beyond their own personal

Greek fighting style

The Greek city-states used a system of citizen-soldiers, with those who could afford a full set of equipment serving as 'hoplites' and those of lesser means making up the supporting arms. A war would take a large proportion of the economically active population away from their businesses, causing significant disruption whether it was won or lost. The solution was a clash of spear-armed phalanxes, often at a traditional or prearranged spot on the routes between the two warring city-states. The clash of phalanxes would produce a decisive result in a short time, enabling the survivors of both sides to return home quickly while a treaty was agreed.

Phalanx warfare was used to settle the disputes of the city-states until the end of the Classical period. This came about largely as a result of the disruption and weakness caused by the costly Peloponnesian War, which allowed the neighbouring kingdom of Macedon to take control of the Greek city-states.

self-interest. Someone who only minded his own business was considered useless in Athenian society.

Athens was not the only city-state to practice democracy, although some had more traditional oligarchical forms of government. In any case, no matter how democratic a city-state's internal affairs might be, politics involving other states and their citizens were robust. Conflict was not uncommon, and the need to resolve a war quickly resulted in a uniquely Greek style of warfare.

The Hellenistic Era and the Eclipse of Greece

The rise of Macedonia began under the rule of Philip II, who modified the phalanx to make it a more flexible formation and implemented cooperation with cavalry and other troops. His armies fought successful campaigns in Greece and the surrounding lands, bringing them into his empire. Upon his

BELOW: Alexander the Great built upon the strengths of the Greek phalanx by integrating it with other troops into a cohesive force. With this army he conquered a vast empire and constructed several cities named after himself.

BELOW: The Battle of Corinth marked the eclipse of Greece and the dominance of Rome. Yet Rome was originally part of the Greek world and was heavily influenced during its development, making this an evolution rather than an ending.

assassination in 336BC, Philip II was succeeded by his son, Alexander – later known as Alexander the Great.

It has been claimed that Alexander was in fact fathered by the king of the gods, Zeus. He was certainly tutored by the great philosopher Aristotle. His was a heroic style of leadership that produced great but short-lived conquests. His army carved out an empire stretching across Persia to India, but it rapidly fragmented after his death in 323BC. The successors of Alexander the Great were not cast in the same mould. They claimed segments of his former empire in Greece, Egypt and Persia, but none could reach far enough to grab Alexander's whole legacy.

The Hellenistic era of Greek history began in conflict, as Alexander's successors fought one another or made shifting alliances to defeat a rival. By 275BC, these conflicts were over, although the kingdom of Macedon continued to fight major rivals in the Greek world including Sparta and alliances of other major city-states.

The rising power of Rome challenged the states of Greece, leading to conflict that ended in 146BC with the Battle of Corinth. The more flexible Roman style of warfare defeated the Greek phalanx, ultimately breaking Greek power. However, by this time, the heartlands of Greece were not the only centres of the Greek world. Egypt was essentially a Greek kingdom as a result of conquest by Alexander's armies. Sicily was also a major Greek stronghold. Syracuse was originally founded on Sicily by colonists from Corinth. It had been fought over by Sparta and Athens and eventually emerged as one of the great centres of the Greek world. Syracuse sided with Carthage against Rome and became a major battleground of the Punic Wars. Despite defences masterminded by the great inventor Archimedes, Syracuse eventually fell to Rome.

Other Greek possessions were taken by the expanding Roman state. Massalia (modern Marseille) was constructed to support trade in the western Mediterranean, and remained an important port and trading centre long after Greece had faded from prominence. It was eventually caught up in Roman politics and was captured in 49BC during the civil war that would in time lead to Rome becoming an empire.

Rome itself is said to have been founded by Greeks fleeing the Trojan Wars, and in its early years was very Greek in character. The early Roman army was organized on a phalanx basis, although this proved unsuitable for the mountainous terrain that its early enemies inhabited. Rome evolved from a Greek offshoot into a culture in its own right, although it retained many aspects of Greek culture. Many Roman gods are identical to Greek deities in all but name, and Apollo is common to both cultures.

Greek Legacy in the Ancient World

Greek influences continued to be felt throughout the Mediterranean region long after the city-states and colonies became possessions of Rome. Indeed, Norsemen seeking adventure in the service of the Byzantine Empire referred to the whole eastern Mediterranean as 'Greece', and the term 'Greek' is often used for the Byzantine Empire. This was a remnant of the Roman Empire, but the Greek association seems to have outlasted the rule of Rome.

Of course, by the time of the Byzantine Empire, the deities of ancient Greece were no longer worshipped; Christianity and Islam vied for supremacy in the Mediterranean region. However, the legends of the old gods and heroes lived on and influenced the mythology of other peoples even to the present day.

ABOVE: Along with Iris, goddess of the rainbow, Apollo retained his Greek name when worshipped by the Romans. While associated with laws and wisdom, Apollo was a rather jealous and bad-tempered god at times.

1

COSMOLOGY AND CREATION

The Ancient Greeks, like other contemporary societies, were polytheists whose gods represented aspects of the physical universe as well as being personifications of attitudes and emotions. Their gods were not the creators of the universe, but overthrew their predecessors to assume dominance of the universe.

This is a common theme in ancient religions, often representing the rise of a society at the expense of its predecessor. Thus, the struggle of the Greek gods against the Titans may represent the overthrow of an earlier culture or the development of Ancient Greek culture from chaotic origins.

The physical cosmos

The Ancient Greeks originally believed that the world was flat or perhaps cylindrical, but over time this view was challenged. Scientific observations of phenomena such as the curvature of the horizon permitted a reasonably accurate calculation of the

OPPOSITE: **The infant Zeus was hidden from his father, Chronos the Titan, among the nymphs of Mount Ida on Crete. The Kouretes concealed the sounds Zeus made with drumming and the clash of weapons in their martial dances.**

Earth's diameter to be made by around 230BC, and long before this the 'round Earth theory' was commonly accepted.

Pythagoras (c.571–497BC) is credited with putting forward the concept that the Earth was spherical. His reasons may not have been altogether scientific, however. The Ancient Greeks considered that the circle was the most perfect of geometrical shapes and the sphere was therefore the perfect embodiment of an object. It followed that the world should be spherical, and so should the surrounding cosmos, and that circular motion was inherently good. Thus, the spherical earth stood at the centre of a spherical cosmos, and other bodies such as the sun and planets moved around it. This concept is credited to Aristotle (c.384–322BC), and remained the accepted view of the cosmos for centuries.

Plato (c.427–347BC) postulated that the world was made up of four elements – earth, air, fire and water – that were divided out of the primordial chaos of the universe by divine means by the demiurge, or creator-god. Aristotle added a fifth element to these: aether. Aether was an otherworldly form of matter, making up the structure of bodies such as the sun and stars. This concept permitted these heavenly bodies to move in their circular paths across the sky without contradicting the four-earthly-elements model of terrestrial phenomena.

ABOVE: The ancient poet Hesiod was sufficiently well respected by the Roman civilization that they copied Greek busts of him. This example was found near Auch, in southwestern France.

Religion and Science

Other philosophers and scientists, such as Epicurus (c.342–271BC), put forward hypotheses that contradicted this accepted view. Epicurus suggested that the building blocks of the universe were not four or five elements, but a much more diverse set of substances, which he called 'atoms' that could be combined to create compounds. He also proposed that the cosmos was infinite (and thus not spherical) and contained many worlds. Aristarchus (c.310–230BC) suggested that the sun might be the centre of the cosmos rather than the earth.

All these ideas were based on physical observations and rational thought, but the idea that the elements were defined by gods and the universe set in motion by them in no way conflicted with the scientific mindset of the Ancient Greeks. They were conducting a scientific examination of a universe where gods were real and powerful, and where an otherwise unexplained phenomenon could be attributed to the actions or creations of a god.

Chaos and the Primordial Gods

Several versions of the creation story exist. The earliest is attributed to the poet Hesiod, a contemporary of Homer. Some time around 700BC, Hesiod published his Theogony, which is probably a compilation and an attempt at rationalization of the many creation stories being told at the time. Hesiod put forward the idea that the primordial gods were created from Chaos. Other sources present different origins for the universe, although many elements are common to several versions.

In the Chaos-origin mythology, before the creation of the cosmos there was only Chaos, an unknowable state consisting of formless primal energy and the potential for all things. Ancient Greek sources disagree on the nature of Chaos, which is fitting given its existence outside the perception and experience of mortals. Chaos is considered one of the primordial gods by some Ancient Greek writers, but this is not universal. Even its name can vary. Chaos is sometimes translated as 'void', but this does not imply emptiness so much as formlessness. Chaos is 'void' in the sense that it contains nothing of use to mortals; nothing yet formed into a recognizable state.

Chaos was an infinite well of possibilities containing the stuff from which the universe was created, and from it came the first three primordial gods: Gaea, Eros and Tartarus.

Gaea, mother of all creation in some versions of the story, was the earth, Tartarus was the underworld and Eros was love. Once Eros existed, it became possible for the primordial gods to procreate. In some versions of the creation myth, Chaos and Gaea, both represented as female, had a child named Erebus, who was the darkness. In other versions, Erebus was the child of Chaos alone.

BELOW: Gaea is sometimes considered to be the source of all creation, rather than the formless void of Chaos. The ideas that everything sprang from the mother earth or that the earth was formed from a primordial wellspring of creation are equally valid.

Nyx was also a child of Chaos. She was the night, and different from Erebus the darkness. Nyx was extremely powerful, but largely inactive once she had mothered several notable children including Thanatos (death), Hypnos (sleep) and the three Fates. According to some versions of the tale, Nyx and Erebus were the parents of Aether (the brightness in the upper air) and Hemera (day).

Gaea gave birth to Uranus (the sky or heavens) and Pontus (the ocean). In Hesiod's Theogony, both were conceived without the assistance of any other gods, although some sources cite Aether as the father. Uranus became Gaea's husband, and fathered many of the major figures in Greek mythology.

RIGHT: Nyx, the primordial goddess of night, was the mother of many frightening beings including Thanatos (death). Her place in the Greek pantheon represents the primal fear of the darkness and what might lurk in it.

The children of Gaea and Uranus include the three Cyclopes, who served as workers for the gods; the three mighty Hecatoncheires who created earthquakes and ocean waves; and the Titans. Other children of Gaea, conceived without the assistance of Uranus, were the Ourea. These were notable mountains including Olympus.

Pontus is primarily associated with the Mediterranean Sea, although after the ascension of Poseidon to rule the oceans he faded from importance. His wife was Thalassa, daughter of Aether and Hemera, and together they populated the seas with all manner of marine life. Pontus also had children with Gaea, including Nereus, father of water nymphs, and Thaumas, who personified the mix of fascination and dread with which the seas are often viewed.

Khronos and Ananke

In other versions of the creation myth, the gods Khronos (time) and Ananke (compulsion, or inevitability) existed at the beginning of all things. The role of Chaos as the wellspring of all creation is taken by the cosmic egg, which was used by Khronos and Ananke to form the universe. Their first creation was Phanes, the progenitor of life, or life processes such as reproduction.

This is in many ways a more scientific view than Hesiod's version. If 'inevitability' is translated as the immutable laws of thermodynamics, which govern energy transfers and thus all the processes of the universe, then everything was created by a set of physical laws (Ananke) and sufficient time (Khronos) to allow them to run their course.

The existence of Khronos as a primordial god in some versions of the Ancient Greek cosmology and as a Titan in others can be confusing. This is not the only occasion where some sources place a particular being in a very different part of the mythical chronology. In some sources, Eros is one of the primordial gods whose existence makes possible much of the creation myth, but

ABOVE: In some versions of Greek mythology, Phanes was the god of creation who hatched from the cosmic egg. Rulership of the universe passed from Phanes to Nyx then to Uranus and finally Zeus.

is the son of Aphrodite in others. This places his appearance several cosmic generations later than Hesiod's version.

The first primordial gods, those born directly of Chaos, can be considered the initial generation of deities in Ancient Greek cosmology, with their children as the second. They represent fundamental concepts in the universe such as the earth and sky, darkness and the oceans. Subsequent generations of gods tend to be more specialized, usually gaining some aspects of their nature from their parent or parents.

The primordial gods did not directly interact with the world to any great extent. They were the driving forces of the universe, exerting influence rather than wandering about the mortal world causing mayhem as subsequent generations of gods would do. The next generation of deities, known as the Titans, permitted their own downfall by their internal squabbles, but in the meantime they were the first divine beings to rule the world rather than shaping it.

Mythical cosmology

The actions of the primordial gods resulted in a cosmos whose form remains more or less the same throughout Greek mythology. Early sources differ on some of the details, however – both with each other and also internally from time to time. Some sources contradict themselves on the location of regions, or use different names for the same place.

Homer's mythical world-view represented the earth as a flat disc surrounded by and floating on the world-river Okeanos. The seas of the world partially covered the land but were not part of the boundary river. The heavens were held up by pillars at the edges of the world, known as the Pillars of Heaven, while the Pillars of Earth lay deeper even than the underworld and supported the lands of the surface world.

OPPOSITE: The Titan Chronos represented the changes which occur over time rather than 'being' time itself. He ruled over the Golden Age in which mortals were closest to the gods, and afterwards humanity became increasingly degenerate.

BELOW: A map of the world according to Homer, around 700BC. Legendary places such as Hyperborea lie just beyond the regions explored by mortals, and all things are surrounded by the world-river Okeanos.

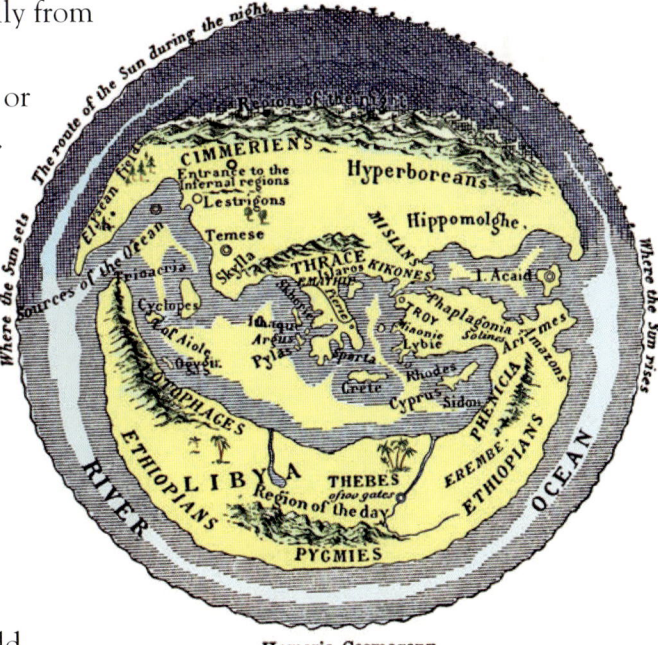

Homeric Cosmogony.

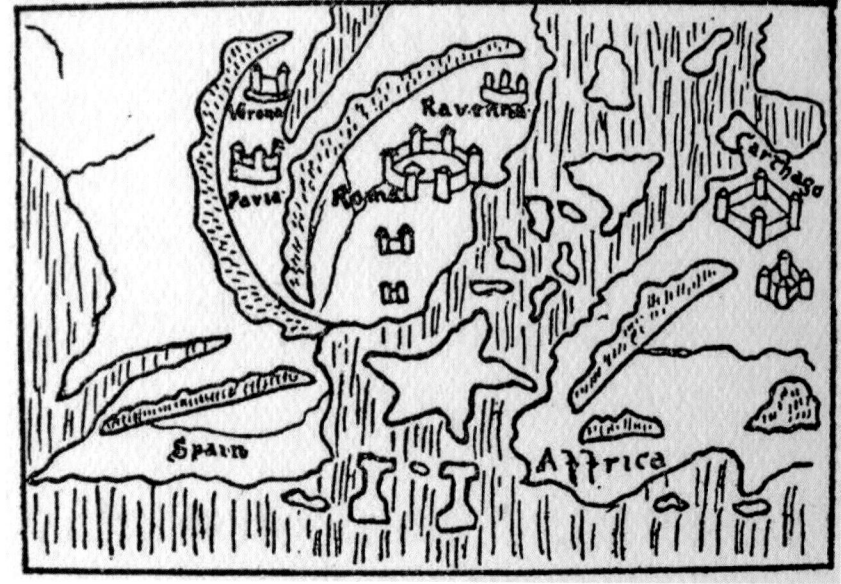

RIGHT: An Anglo-Saxon map of the entrance to the Mediterranean, dating from the 10th century AD. The Pillars of Hercules are marked, along with major cities and very approximate locations of major islands.

Above the earth was the aether, the bright upper sky, and above that lay the heavens. The dividing line between the heavens and the aether was the orbit of the moon. Anything higher than this followed celestial circular motion; anything below obeyed the rules of the earth as inhabited by mortals.

The heavens consisted of a set of spheres, one inside the next, which rotated. The stars were fixed to the outermost sphere and all moved together, accounting for the fact that they did not move relative to one another. Planets were each attached to their own sphere and moved separately to one another and to the stars. The word 'planet' is derived from Ancient Greek; it meant 'wanderer' and referred to the fact that planets behaved differently from stars.

The mortal realm

All the lands and seas explored by the Ancient Greeks were contained within the disc of the mortal realm. Some locations had their own significance, such as mountains or rivers associated with a god or spirit. Others were important in their own right. The mouth of the world-river Okeanos was located somewhere to the north of the Pillars of Hercules (the western entrance to the Mediterranean), from where it flowed around the lands where mortals lived. Some sources place Tartarus on the surface, far to the northwest of Greece on the shores of Okeanos. It is not clear why this reference is made when Tartarus is almost always accepted as being deep in the underworld.

The Ancient Greeks were great maritime explorers, whose ships ranged up and down the Mediterranean. They knew about far-off places, but of course some of what they knew had passed into legend. Accounts of voyages to very distant areas such as the western end of the Mediterranean Sea were more than likely embellished to the point of being legends in their own right, and some of these far-off places probably had stories associated with them dating from before the Greek Dark Age.

At the western end of the Mediterranean, according to Greek legend, were the Pillars of Hercules. The northern one is identifiable as the Rock of Gibraltar. The southern pillar was one of the peaks on the coast of North Africa, but it is not certain which one. Greek tradition held that the passage between the pillars led out on to the vast expanse of Okeanos, with no far shore. The idea that the pillars were inscribed in Latin with 'ne plus ultra', signifying that there was nothing beyond them, originated during the Renaissance, although the concept that this was essentially the end of the world did exist in Ancient Greek times.

THE LOCATION OF ATLANTIS

According to Plato, the lost civilization of Atlantis lay beyond the Pillars of Hercules, although this may have been a poetic reference to it being lost somewhere out in the vast seas of the world rather than a specific reference. It remains unclear whether Plato believed his tale of an advanced society whose homeland vanished beneath the seas. His Atlantis may have been a metaphor for Greek society or an echo of the vanished Minoan civilization. There are no legends of gods or heroes journeying to Atlantis, making it debatable whether Atlantis belongs within the Ancient Greek mythological cosmology or should be considered a poetic metaphor invented to make a philosophical point. If Atlantis did lie beyond the Pillars of Hercules, it was outside the realms accessible to mortals even if it were not sunk at the bottom of the ocean.

BELOW: **The lost continent of Atlantis.**

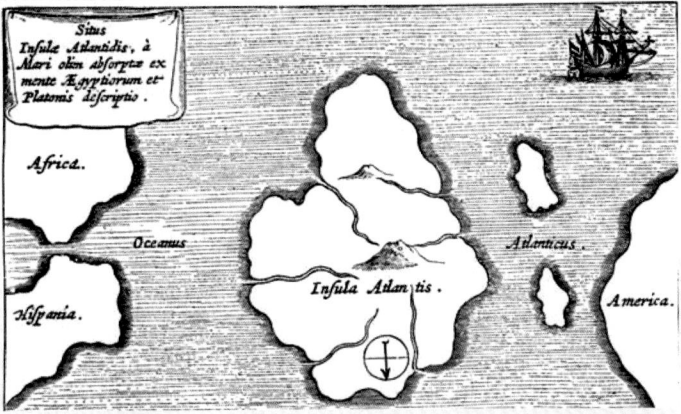

Semi-mythical geography

All around the Mediterranean lay many islands, some of them inhabited by friends of Greece and some by enemies. Many were entirely unexplored, and accurate charts were hard to come by. It was not hard to imagine that among those islands lay fabulous

lands and the homes of monsters. Similarly, the lands around the Mediterranean were inhabited by other civilizations and by 'barbarians' – called thus because, according to the Ancient Greeks, their speech consisted of unintelligible 'bar-bar-bar' noises.

BELOW: Some aspects of Eratosthenes' map of the world are reasonably accurate, though other areas are clearly based on distorted hearsay.

Garbled accounts of these people and their own legends as recounted to Greek explorers contributed to the Ancient Greek world-view, mixing real knowledge with accepted myth to create a semi-mythical map of the Mediterranean world. Legendary events took place in real places, or perhaps distorted versions of real places.

At the northeast corner of the Aegean Sea lay the Bosporus, a narrow seaway giving access to the Black Sea and all the lands around it. These were dangerous waters, with many islands and turbulent currents making navigation hazardous. The cities along the eastern coast of the Mediterranean and around the Black Sea were trading destinations for Greek ships, and will have been visited by earlier mariners such as the Minoans. Again, these places would be both the source of distorted tales and a setting for legendary events.

Among these cities was the legendary Troy, the setting for Homer's *Iliad*. Homer was writing on the other side of the Greek

BELOW: Archaeological excavations have revealed a succession of cities standing on the site of Troy. This does not prove that Homer's account of the siege was factual, but it does suggest the story may have been based on real events.

Dark Age from the events he was describing, but cities in that region were destroyed by raiders from the sea during the Bronze Age collapse, and were the scene of conflict at other times. Such places became part of the Ancient Greek mythological cosmology; partly remembered histories melding with legendary events.

Thus, the Ancient Greek image of their world was a mix of knowledge and myth. It is hard for today's observer to see where one ends and the other begins. For a citizen of those times, the distinction may have been irrelevant. Their gods walked in these places and their heroes performed their great deeds there. The fact that sailors had visited the places mentioned in the legends may have made them all the more believable.

We cannot know for certain whether the average Ancient Greek mariner worried about monsters living on the island ahead, or if tales of mystical beasts and magical threats were taken at face value. But ships did go missing, and dire legends of monsters might serve as useful warnings to stay away from certain places. They might also provide an explanation of the fate of a missing ship. It is possible that an ancient mariner might be just as worried about sirens or clashing rocks as about pirates or adverse currents. Propitiating the gods to protect against these dangers was undoubtedly seen as a wise precaution.

The underworld

The deepest part of the underworld was Tartarus, where monsters and those who had offended the gods were imprisoned. The region of Tartarus was associated with the primordial god of the same name, just as the surface world was associated with Gaea. The term 'Tartarus' is sometimes used to refer to the whole of the underworld, although commonly other regions have their own identity.

Hades, named after the Titan who ruled it, lay between earth and Tartarus. It was part of the underworld but was not as terrifying as Tartarus. All mortal things went to Hades after death, where judgement was passed and punishment conferred upon those who deserved it. According to Hesiod, Hades lay so far below the earth that an anvil would take nine days to fall from the surface to Hades. Tartarus lay another nine days' fall below.

ABOVE: Most of what we know about Tartarus comes from the adventures of heroes who journeyed there. When Odysseus visited Tartarus he encountered Achilles, who lamented that he would rather be a poor live man than a ruler in the land of the dead.

Not all the dead went to Hades or Tartarus. Those of exceptional worth were permitted to enter the Fields of Elysium; in later versions, this privilege seems to have been extended to those who were good and decent in a more mundane way. Elysium appears in Homer's works, while Hesiod refers to the Isles of the Blessed in the same way. Both are located somewhere in the ocean at the west of the world.

The birth of the Titans

The Titans were the children of heaven and earth, personified by Uranus and Gaea. Like the Olympian gods who came after them, the Titans were frequently at odds with one another. They were not the first children of Uranus and Gaea; before them came the three cyclopes and the three Hecatoncheires, giants of great power named Briareos, Kottos and Gye. They each had 50 heads and 100 hands, and frightened Uranus with their power.

Briareos eventually married Poseidon's daughter and became associated with the Aegean Sea. In this guise he is often known

The rivers of the underworld

In order to enter Hades, the dead were required to cross one of its five rivers: the Styx. Those who could not afford to pay the ferryman were forced to linger on the banks of the Styx – either forever, as in some versions, or for a century. The Styx was by far the greatest of the rivers of the underworld, containing one-tenth of the waters of the world-river Okeanos. The river was personified by a goddess of the same name, who was the first of the many daughters of Okeanos. Perhaps due to its status as the barrier between the worlds of the living and the dead, the Styx had great significance. An oath sworn on the Styx could bind even a god, with severe consequences if it were broken, and the waters of the Styx could impart invulnerability.

The other rivers all had their own significance. The Lethe flowed around the cave of Hypnos (sleep) and imparted forgetfulness upon those who drank from it. According to some myths, souls could be reincarnated but only after they drank from the Lethe to forget their former lives. It was necessary to cross the river Lethe in order to enter Elysium.

The river Cocytus, representing lamentation, does not play a large part in the Ancient Greek cosmology. Nor does Phlegethon, the river of fire. Both feature in much later works such as Milton's *Paradise Lost* and Dante's *Inferno*. The Acheron, river of woe, is less important than the Styx in early sources, but serves as a source of purification for sinners and those seeking absolution.

As with other myths, the significance of the rivers of Hades varied over time. In early versions, the five rivers of Hades – the Styx, Acheron, Cocytus, Phlegethon and Lethe – all flow together to create a marsh in the centre of Hades. The marsh was named Styx, indicating the pre-eminence of that river. According to Virgil, a Roman poet writing much later than Homer or Hesiod, the river Acheron was a barrier to the newly dead, who were ferried across it by the boatman Charon. It was the source of the Styx and the Cocytus, although Homer states that the Cocytus and Phlegethon were tributaries of the Acheron.

BELOW: **Charon ferrying souls across the Styx.**

ABOVE: **The works of Victorian painter George Frederic Watts included several scenes from Greek mythology. His representation of the Titans was influenced by his study of the classics at an early age.**

as Aigaion. His two brothers became guardians of Tartarus. Perhaps Uranus was right to be wary of his mighty offspring, but in his fear he tried to push them back inside Gaea's womb, which did not endear him to his wife. Despite this incident, Uranus and Gaea produced more children, who would be the downfall of Uranus. These were the twelve Titans.

Other versions of the tale suggest that Gaea wearied of Uranus' all-encompassing embrace. As the heavens he could enfold her on all sides, which had seemed desirable at first. Later, Gaea wished to be rid of her overly amorous husband and conspired with her Titan children to dispose of him.

There were six male Titans and six females. Their name means 'stretchers' or 'strainers', in reference to their lack of self-restraint. The Titans did as they pleased with no thought as to the consequences for themselves or for anyone else. Uranus is portrayed as cruel and oppressive, although perhaps he was merely trying to rein in the conduct of his powerful and wilful children.

The Titans' father turns against them

The Titans' behaviour worried their father, who banished them to Tartarus, deep within Gaea. This caused her grave suffering, but Uranus still wanted to mate with her. Unwilling to be forced to keep yet more children inside her, Gaea asked the Titans for help. Five of the six males were too frightened of Uranus to assist their mother, but Chronos was willing.

Gaea fashioned a magical sickle; some versions of the story credit her with inventing flint to make the weapon. Chronos ambushed Uranus when he came to lie with Gaea, castrating his father, whose genitals fell into the sea. From them was born Aphrodite, goddess of love. The blood that fell on the land was absorbed by Gaea, who produced more children as a result. These included the Erinyes, or Furies, and the Gigantes who would later war with the Olympian gods.

The castration of Uranus had two major effects. One was to separate the earth and the heavens, and ensure that Gaea did not produce any more children. The other was to establish Chronos as the leader and king of the Titans, effectively making him ruler of the cosmos. He took Mount Olympus as his home, driving out Eurynome (a daughter of Okeanos) and her husband Ophion. Some sources suggest that Eurynome and Ophion were rulers of the world before Chronos deposed them; in other versions they seem to be fairly minor deities.

Chronos freed the three Hecatoncheires from Gaea's womb at last, but was dismayed by their power just as his father Uranus had been. Fearing he might be overthrown in turn, Chronos imprisoned the three brothers within the earth. He took his sister, and fellow Titan, Rhea as his wife – although he was not faithful to her and, despite the lessons to be learned from the fate of Uranus, Chronos began to father children.

ABOVE: The castration of Uranus by Chronos. According to some versions of the story, Gaea created flint to make a weapon capable of harming her husband, suggesting that no suitable material had previously existed.

Attempting to imprison the children inside their mother had obviously failed Uranus, so Chronos decided he would swallow them himself. He did so with his first five children, but Rhea found a way to spare the sixth this fate. Substituting a rock wrapped in baby clothes for the infant, Rhea sent the child to be hidden away on the island of Crete. There, he was raised by nymphs and protected by warrior spirits named Kouretes. They prevented Chronos from hearing the baby by making a great deal of noise with their weapons and shields whenever he cried.

This child was Zeus, and he would eventually overthrow his father just as Chronos had feared. In the meantime, he grew to adulthood in secrecy, and Chronos continued to behave with Titanic abandon. He had at least one affair, with a daughter of Okeanos named Philyra, and was almost caught with her by his wife Rhea. To avoid discovery, Chronos turned himself into a horse, and the resulting offspring was Kheiron, the first centaur.

ABOVE: **Zeus was Romanized as Jupiter, and it is likely that at first his stories were unchanged. As Roman society diverged from its Greek roots, its chief god evolved to be the patron of the new state.**

The first-generation Titans

The twelve first-generation Titans are known as the Uranides, the children of Uranus and Gaea. Some of them formed brother–sister partnerships and produced children of varying importance. Not all of the first-generation Titans fought against Zeus and his kin, instead taking a place in the new Olympian pantheon or continuing in their original role without any real interruption.

In some versions of the tale, Chronos was assisted by four of his brothers, who were positioned at the corners of the world to seize and hold Uranus while Chronos castrated him. The brothers thus became associated with the pillars that held the heavens aloft.

The first-born of the Titans was Okeanos, associated with the world-river that surrounds the mortal realm. In most versions of the story, Okeanos remained neutral or aloof from the conflicts of Titans and gods. He declined to help Chronos against Uranus, and did not fight against Zeus and the Olympians.

The wife of Okeanos was Tethys, a daughter of Gaea. She was the mother of rivers and of the nymphs associated with bodies of water. Tethys plays a very minor part in Greek myth, mainly as a source of waters and clouds, although she is sometimes portrayed as a vastly more powerful deity who – depending on the version – was one of the creators of the universe or co-ruler of the cosmos. In the latter guise she is equated with Eurynome, who was overthrown by the Titan Chronos and driven out of Olympus.

Hyperion was the Titan associated with the lights of heaven, while his wife Theia was associated with shining objects, notably gold, and the brightness of the aether. Their children were Eos, the dawn; Helios, the sun; and Selene, the moon. Hyperion was one of the four male Titans who assisted Chronos against Uranus (Okeanos was the only one who did not) and was probably associated with the easternmost of the four pillars of heaven.

Helios, the sun, lived at the far eastern edge of the world in a golden palace. Each day he drove his chariot across the sky

BELOW: Most surviving depictions of ancient gods are in the form of pottery, statues or mosaics such as this one depicting Okeanos and Tethys. Okeanos remained neutral during the great conflicts of the Olympians and Titans.

RIGHT: Eos, goddess of the dawn, is often depicted riding a chariot similar to that used by her brother Helios. Like many of the younger Titans, Eos was co-opted into the Olympian pantheon without conflict.

towards the lands of the Hesperides in the far west, descending into the world-ocean at dusk. From there he sailed home during the night in a golden bowl, ready to rise again in the morning.

The rise of Helios was prepared each day by his sister Eos, who burned away the morning mists with her rays. Like some of the other Titans, Eos is associated with one of the primordial deities. In this case, Eos has much in common with Hemera, goddess of day, just as Chronos is associated with and has similar abilities to Khronos, primordial god of time. There is no indication that these Titans were reincarnations or personifications of the primordial gods; the similarities are more likely the result of generations of myths with different focuses but a need for similar characters.

Eos is sometimes depicted as riding a chariot drawn by winged horses, and on other occasions as flying on wings of her own. She had a weakness for handsome young men, taking many lovers, and this did not always work out well. After joining the Olympian pantheon, Eos asked Zeus to make her lover Tithonus, a prince of Troy, immortal. Zeus agreed, but did not grant eternal youth along with longevity. Tithonus aged but could not die, eventually becoming a grasshopper.

The third child of Hyperion and Theia was Selene, the moon. Like her siblings, Selene was a charioteer, although she had two winged horses where Helios had four. Selene is also depicted as riding a horse or driving a herd of oxen. She, like her sister Eos, took a mortal lover but fared better. Zeus allowed Selene's lover Endymion to sleep forever, retaining his youth and beauty, while Selene visited him each night. Other legends of Endymion make him a patron of horse-racing who settled the question of succession among his heirs with a race before dying. These legends have a different source to the stories of the Titans, resulting in one of the many contradictions found within Greek mythology.

The first-generation Titans Coeus and Phoebe, representing intellect and wisdom respectively, played little part in the affairs of the gods and Titans after Coeus helped overthrow Uranus, but were passively responsible for knowledge and learning. Phoebe was mother to Leto – mother by Zeus of Apollo and Artemis – and Asteria, who is named as the mother of Hecate by different fathers depending on the version of the myth.

Both these female Titans lived in Olympus after the overthrow of their parents' generation, and both were the subject of Zeus' advances. Asteria fled from him in the form of a quail, eventually falling into the sea to become a floating island. This in turn provided a refuge for her sister Leto, who was pregnant with Zeus' children Apollo and Artemis. Fleeing the wrath of Hera, Zeus' vengeful wife, Leto was forbidden to set foot on land, but since the island she found – later identified as Delos – was not connected to the seabed it was technically not land and thus the only place where she could give birth to her children.

Chronos, although the youngest of the male Titans, became their leader due to his overthrow of Uranus. With his wife Rhea he had important children including Zeus, Poseidon and Hades. Chronos led the Titans in their war against the Olympians when Zeus rebelled against him. Had circumstances been different, perhaps Zeus and his siblings might have been considered Titans rather than Olympian gods.

BELOW: The Titaness Leto, one of Zeus' many lovers, became pregnant with the twins Apollo and Artemis. Although their mother was a Titan, as were all their grandparents, Artemis and Apollo were very much Olympian gods.

The second-generation Titans

Foremost among the second generation of Titans were the four Iapetionides, named for their father Iapetus. Iapetus was the Titan associated with mortal life, craftsmanship and the westernmost of the Pillars of Heaven. He did not form a partnership with one of the first-generation female Titans but instead took Clymene as his wife. Clymene was a daughter of Okeanos and might be

BELOW: The torment of Prometheus was depicted in Rubens' painting Prometheus Bound, begun in 1611 or 1612 and completed by the end of the decade.

considered a lesser being than a first-generation Titan, but their children Prometheus, Epimetheus, Atlas and Menoetius were extremely powerful and important.

Prometheus was a great benefactor to humankind, although he suffered terribly for it. He stole fire from Olympus and gave it to humans, and for this was badly punished by Zeus. Prometheus was chained to a rock for eagles to gnaw at his liver, which was endlessly renewed until he was finally rescued by the hero Heracles.

Epimetheus was less openly defiant, but brought great misery upon the world by opening the box belonging to Pandora whom he had taken as his wife. Atlas, associated with strength and endurance, and Menoetius, associated with violence and rash actions, fought against Zeus alongside Chronos and were punished for it. Atlas was condemned to hold up the heavens and Menoetius was imprisoned in Tartarus.

Mnemosyne, a first-generation female Titan, was associated with time and memory. She became a patron of the preservation of knowledge through stories and histories, and sometimes pronounced prophecies. After the overthrow of Chronos, Mnemosyne was a lover of Zeus, giving birth to the Muses who inspired art, songs and dance.

Likewise, Themis did not take another Titan as her husband. After the overthrow of Chronos she was a lover of Zeus, becoming mother to the Horae (seasons) and Moirae (fates). In her own right she was a lawgiver who taught humanity about morality and law as well as the proper respect for and offerings to the gods.

Krios was associated with the constellations and probably the southernmost of the Pillars of Heaven. He was cast into Tartarus when the Titans were overthrown. Krios took as his wife a daughter of Pontus, Eurybia, who represented mastery over the seas. Their descendants were extremely important in the affairs of humans.

Astraios, husband of Eos, fathered the stars and the seasonal winds. Perses, Titan of destruction, fathered Hecate, the mother of witchcraft, upon Asteria. Pallas, associated with war, was the husband of Styx and the father of Nike (victory),

BELOW: Hecate, Titan goddess of witchcraft and magic was also associated with crossroads. This is perhaps the origin of the popular 'crossroads bargain' with dark forces which exists in several cultures. Hecate is often depicted in triplicate.

Kratos (strength), Bia (power) and Zelos (rivalry). His children fought alongside Zeus and the Olympians, participating in the overthrow of the Titans.

The overthrow of the Titans

Zeus was raised in secrecy, and since he believed he had swallowed all of his children the titan Chronos had no reason to suspect that Zeus was one of his offspring when he presented himself. Zeus found employment in his father's court as a cup-bearer. Given that Chronos had betrayed his own father Uranus, he would surely never have granted such a position of trust if he had had any doubts about Zeus' identity or his intentions.

Zeus had allies within Chronos's court, or at least there were those who were opposed to Chronos and willing to help him. Metis, daughter of Okeanos and Tethys, later became Zeus' wife, so it is possible that she fell in love with him at Chronos's court. Whatever her motivations for helping, Metis provided Zeus with a drink made of mustard and wine, which would make Chronos sick.

THE TITANS IN MYTH

There are few myths dealing directly with the age of the Titans. Many references are part of the backstory in a tale of heroes or Olympian gods, with little reference to the deeds of the Titans outside those stories. In general, the Titans represent an 'old order' that was destroyed by the new Olympian society, but they are not evil in any real sense.

The Greek pantheon is complex, with no simple good-versus-evil divide. Many of the Titans joined the Olympian gods or seem to have continued about their business unaffected by the rise to prominence of the Olympian deities. There are many internal rivalries and enmities among the Titans and the Olympians, and although there are some beings who seem to be permanently at odds, neither is portrayed as 'bad' or 'good' as such. Indeed, the actions of many of the gods are selfish and sometimes quite unpleasant, and there is no real suggestion that the Olympians somehow protect humanity from the return of the bad old days.

Instead, the age of the Titans resulted in a world where humans could live and prosper, with maritime navigation made possible by the winds and the constellations, with a cycle of days and seasons that allowed crops to be planted and harvested. The natural order of things was established in the age of the Titans, and even when they were overthrown the pattern of day and night, the rise of the constellations and the seasonal change of the winds was not greatly altered. The rise of the Olympians did have some profound effects on the world, however, mainly due to the jealousies and endless squabbling among themselves.

The drink must have been very powerful, as Chronos vomited up all of the children he had swallowed and was unable to prevent Zeus from conspiring with them against him. The war was not won in a day, however. Instead, the future Olympians fought for ten years against their father and his supporters. The conflict became known as the Titanomachy.

Zeus sought other allies, freeing the Cyclopes and Hecatoncheires from their prisons. The Hecatoncheires were very powerful, hurling rocks with their many hands, but for all their physical power the Cyclopes served the gods best as artificers. For Zeus they made thunderbolts, each Cyclops contributing an element of the final weapon – lighting, thunder and brightness.

ABOVE: **The Titanomachy was a suitably epic conflict, in which the Olympians prevailed by obtaining allies among those who had been mistreated by the Titans. Exactly which Titans fought in the war varies from one version to another.**

The Cyclopes also armed Zeus' brothers Poseidon and Hades. For Hades they made a helm of darkness that could render him invisible, and for Poseidon they made a trident. These gifts match the areas of influence the gods gained after the Titanomachy, but Poseidon did not receive overlordship of the seas, nor Hades of the underworld, until the end of the war.

Zeus and the Olympians

At the end of the war, Zeus and his Olympians were the clear victors. They seem to have been content to fight for power rather than against the Titans; those who remained neutral were left alone and some came to live in Olympus, effectively becoming Olympians themselves. The defeated Titans were imprisoned in Tartarus, much as Chronos had done with his own enemies. The Hecatoncheires were given the task of guarding them. In some myths, Zeus eventually pardoned some or all of his former foes and allowed them to dwell in Elysium.

Magical weapons of the gods

The fact that Zeus, Poseidon and Hades were given magical weapons suited to their eventual roles could be seen as the work of fate that bound even the gods, but more likely it occurred because that was the way the myth developed. Poseidon as ruler of the seas wielded a weapon resembling a fish spear, so naturally in the myth where the young Poseidon, a god with no particular area of responsibility, is given a magical weapon then it will be the trident that will someday become his symbol. This probably reflects a rationalization of myths on the part of early writers.

The Cyclopes provided other magical weapons to the gods, making bows for Apollo and Artemis, and were instrumental in the overthrow of the Titans. Two Titans, Themis and Prometheus, fought alongside Zeus, while the others sided with Chronos or remained neutral. For such an enormous conflict there are surprisingly few sources, though many stories draw on the events and outcome of this period to explain the existence of magical weapons or why certain circumstances came to pass.

ABOVE: **Neptune, Poseidon's Roman equivalent, with his trademark trident.**

BELOW: **The fall of the Titans, by Dutch painter Cornelis van Haarlem.**

After the conflict, the cosmos was divided between Zeus, Poseidon and Hades, who drew lots to see who would get which part. Hades was given the underworld and Poseidon the sea, with Zeus becoming king of the gods, the sky and the surface world. For mortals, this was the end of the Golden Age in which they had lived like gods under the rule of – or perhaps simply ignored by – the Titans.

The humans of this Golden Age knew nothing of sorrow and did not have to work. It was always spring and, according to some sources, people aged backwards. At the end of their lives people became spirits known as daemones, who acted as guides and helpers to the living.

In the new age of Olympian rule, there were four seasons in the year and mortals needed to work to support themselves. To populate this world, Zeus decided to create a race of mortals and many species of animals, although this did not quite go according to plan.

The creation of animals and mortals

Zeus asked the female Titan, Themis, to create animals. Themis joined the Olympians after the Titanomachy and was at one time a wife of Zeus. As a lawgiver she was well suited to the task of creating entire ecosystems, and by all accounts did so quickly and efficiently. This resulted in problems for Prometheus, who had been tasked with the creation of mortals.

Prometheus saw that Themis had distributed great gifts among her new animal kingdom, leaving nothing for Prometheus to give humans. He was angry, and decided to gift humans with fire whether the gods liked it or not. Whether Zeus was angry at the theft of fire by Prometheus or simply because he had not been consulted, he ordered that Prometheus be chained to a rock for the rest of eternity, so that birds cold peck out his magically restored liver every day.

Not content with punishing Prometheus for the theft, Zeus decided that humanity had to suffer, too. He chose Prometheus' brother Epimetheus as his instrument. Where Prometheus is normally associated with foresight, Epimetheus is normally characterized as unwise and rash, and is connected with the hard-won wisdom of hindsight.

ABOVE: Pandora was the first mortal woman, and the architect of enormous suffering ever since. This may have been Zeus' intention when he created her, taking revenge upon all of humanity for Prometheus' gift of fire.

Zeus created a woman named Pandora, who had a child named Pyrrha with Epimetheus. They were happy together, but eventually curiosity got the better of them. Pandora had been provided with a box containing a small amount of all the gods' powers, and once opened it unleashed a host of ills upon the world. Opening the box a second time, Pandora and Epimetheus discovered that it contained hope, a small consolation for all the evil they had allowed into the world.

The people of this new era, referred to as the Silver Age by Hesiod, were inferior to those of the preceding Golden Age, but they were still greater than modern mortals. A child could enjoy a century of play before having to become a responsible adult. These mortals offended Zeus by failing to properly respect the gods, so they were destroyed. Thus began what Hesiod calls the Bronze Age, with a new race of warlike mortals made from ash trees.

These mortals also turned out to be unsatisfactory, so Zeus decided to wipe them out with a flood. The only survivors were Pyrrha, daughter of Epimetheus and Pandora, and a man named Deucalion who was the son of Prometheus. Deucalion survived due to his father's foresight. He was advised to build a boat or

BELOW: Deucalion and Pyrrha were the only survivors of the flood that ended the Bronze Age. The new race they created were the heroic and semi-mythical ancestors of the Greeks of Hesiod's time.

chest to survive the coming flood, and with his wife Pyrrha he was able to repopulate the world.

After wisely offering thanks to Zeus for sparing them, the couple were told by an oracle to throw rocks over their shoulders, which became a new race of humans when they struck the ground. These were the people of the Age of Heroes, as Hesiod calls it. It was an age where myth and history began to meet; Hesiod considered the Age of Heroes to be recent history, essentially the era of Mycenae before the Greek Dark Age.

The Iron Age

After the Age of Heroes was the Iron Age. This was not a reference to the use of iron for tools and weapons as such, but to the progression from shining and godly gold through lesser silver and dull bronze to iron, a difficult metal to work with. Humanity degenerated through these ages, except during the Age of Heroes in which people regained some of their former greatness. To Hesiod, the Iron Age was the present time, in which humans were petty, small-minded and prone to evildoing. This age, too, was destined to end when Zeus commanded it.

Thus Hesiod, Homer and other writers of the time presented a mythical chronology beginning with the creation of the universe and the acts of the primordial gods and progressing through divine wars and the degeneration of humanity from a state close to godliness to base mortality. Real places, and in some cases oral traditions of possibly real events, were intermixed with metaphor and legend to create an account of how the present world came to be.

This account provided answers to questions about origins and destiny, life and death, as well as examples of worthy and unworthy behaviour. Yet it was not a moralistic tale or an obvious guide to acceptable behaviour. The creation of the modern – to the Ancient Greeks – world was the result of complex and often selfish actions; actions not very different to those that might be taken by mortals. The gods of Ancient Greece were presented as divine people rather than something infinite. The difference was degree of power, not some perfect and unknowable status. These were capricious and jealous gods whose stories no doubt provided entertainment as well as lessons.

2

THE OLYMPIAN GODS

The term 'Olympian' can be used to refer to the whole pantheon of gods led by Zeus, or specifically to the twelve gods who made up the ruling council that met on Olympus. Most of them also lived on Olympus but others, such as Poseidon, had homes elsewhere.

As is often the case in Greek myth, sources cannot agree on the identities of all twelve Olympians. Some, such as Zeus and Hera, are always included, but others are sometimes omitted.

For example, Hades seems not to have attended the council on many occasions and made his home in the underworld rather than on Olympus. He is not always included among the Olympians, in which case his place is usually taken by Hephaestus. Hestia stood down from the council of Olympus but remained resident on Olympus, with her role on the council taken by Dionysus.

OPPOSITE: **Thetis was one of Zeus' lovers, but upon learning she was destined to bear a child who would be greater than his father, Zeus ordered her to wed the mortal Peleus to whom she bore Achilles.**

BELOW: This statue of Zeus, dating from the second century AD, represents him in familiar kingly style, wise and bearded. This image has persisted down to modern times.

THE RULING COUNCIL OF TWELVE

The candidates for a place among the Olympians, depending on the source, are: Zeus, Hera, Aphrodite, Apollo, Ares, Artemis, Athena, Demeter, Hermes, Poseidon, with Dionysus, Hades, Hephaestus and Hestia sometimes included among them. Many other gods lived on Mount Olympus but were not part of the council of twelve.

The Olympian gods came to power by overthrowing their predecessors – a theme common to several mythologies. The war between the Olympians and the Titans has close parallels to the Norse stories of how Odin led the gods against the Giants to gain control of the cosmos. Like the Giants of Norse mythology, many of the Titans were banished from the mortal world. However, Greek mythology does not predict a final battle against the returning Titans. The Olympians were apparently destined to rule forever.

Zeus, King of the Gods

Zeus was the son of the Titans Chronos and Rhea, and inherited some traits from his father. Just as Chronos was unfaithful to his wife, so too was Zeus. His infidelity, like that of Chronos, was not always carried out in his native form. Chronos accidentally fathered the race of centaurs in this manner, although Zeus greatly outdid his father in terms of the mischief his illegitimate offspring caused.

Zeus is associated with the heavens and the weather, as well as authority, kingliness and wisdom. The latter seems to have been wayward at times; Zeus' many affairs led to trouble within Olympus and out in the wider world. According to Homer, Zeus set the path for every mortal's life by assigning ills and blessings from two urns filled with them. The proportions were decided by Zeus, though there is no indication of how he decided how good or bad someone's life would be. It seems that sometimes Zeus handed out a truly miserable existence to someone just because he felt like it.

Zeus' nature may have been shaped by his early upbringing. Hidden from his father, he was raised on the island of Crete by nymphs and warrior spirits. Zeus learned the need for cunning and guile, and also patience, at an early age. He did not challenge Chronos for supremacy until he had tricked him into releasing Zeus' siblings. Even after adding the powerful Cyclopes and Hecatoncheires to his force, Zeus waited until his magical weapons were ready before launching his campaign.

Zeus knew the value of stacking the odds and making proper preparations, and ultimately this brought him victory over the Titans. However, his reign in Olympus was anything but secure. Angry at the defeat of her children, the Titans, Gaea made a direct intervention in the affairs of the world. This was highly unusual; the primordial gods normally remained aloof.

ABOVE: The *Fall of the Giants* by Guido Reni, painted in 1636–37, depicts Zeus defeating giants with his thunderbolts and tumbling huge stones down on top of them. The poetic record of the Gigantomachy was rather vague, leaving plenty of room for artistic interpretation.

Gaea's many children included the Gigantes, created when Uranus' blood fell on to Gaea's body after he was castrated by Chronos. Some sources say there were one hundred Gigantes, and they are variously described as human in appearance but possessing enormous strength (and size, in some cases) and as monstrous beings with animal features such as serpentine tails or lions' heads.

Zeus and the Gigantomachy

The war between the Gigantes and the Olympians is known as the Gigantomachy, and is conflated by some sources with the Titanomachy. It is possible that some giants fought on the side of the Titans but that their war against Olympus was a separate one. Here, again, Zeus' ability to plan ahead was vital. Many prophecies existed at the time, and Zeus became aware of one that stated that he could only win the coming war if he had a mortal fighting for him.

Zeus' mortal son Heracles was eminently suitable, but Zeus was also aware that Gaea knew of the prophecy. She sought a herb that could make her Gigantes immune to any assault by mortals.

This would negate Heracles and tip the balance of the war. However, Zeus got there first and denied Gaea her secret weapon.

Even so, the Gigantomachy was a hard-fought contest in which the Olympians came close to defeat. After they had prevailed, Gaea sent the monstrous giant Typhon against them. Typhon is described as a volcano-giant who would spew fire from his mouth and hurl red-hot rocks at his enemies. Some sources also give him 200 hands with serpents for fingers, and 99 bestial heads in addition to his human one.

Even after narrowly defeating Typhon, Zeus faced dissent and rebellion in Olympus. This was at least partly his own fault; Zeus was wilful and proud, and antagonized the other gods on several occasions. The Titan Prometheus, now living in Olympus, stole fire to give to mortals and was savagely punished for it, but the greatest challenge Zeus faced was from his own kin.

Tiring of his wilfulness – and probably his infidelity – Zeus' wife Hera led a revolt against him. The gods stole Zeus' thunderbolt while he was asleep, and bound him with 100-knotted cords. Sources disagree on exactly which gods were involved in the revolt. In some cases it seems to be more or less the entire population of Olympus other than the nymph Thetis.

Unable to challenge the massed gods directly, Thetis summoned one of the Hecatoncheires, Briareos. Briareos was loyal to Zeus, and perhaps saw the chance to repay him for releasing the Hecatoncheires from Tartarus. Briareos' 100 hands were able to undo the knots binding Zeus before the gods could intervene. Once freed, he was again master of Olympus. Zeus punished Hera and her allies for their treachery, securing his rule over the gods.

The Wives and Children of Zeus

Zeus' first wife was the Titan Metis. Metis was an Oceanid, one of the 3000 daughters of Okeanos and Tethys. The young god had little to offer her when they met; indeed, being associated with him was risky since his father, Chronos, saw Zeus and his siblings as a serious threat. Yet Metis took the enormous risk of helping Zeus infiltrate the court of the Titans and supplying him with the poisoned drink he used to make Chronos vomit out Zeus' siblings.

OPPOSITE: The giant Typhon was perhaps the most fearsome foe the Olympians faced. He wounded Zeus, and in some versions of the story held him captive for a time. He was eventually defeated and imprisoned under Mount Etna.

Zeus and the birth of Athena

Once Zeus was established as the ruler of Olympus, he took Metis as his wife. Their partnership was, according to Hesiod, one of equals, and Metis provided Zeus with wise counsel. Zeus' own wisdom led him to take note of prophecies, and one about his wife concerned him greatly. According to the prophecy, Metis would bear him two children, and the second of them would surpass Zeus. Worried that he would be overthrown as he had overthrown Chronos, Zeus resorted to similar measures. He convinced Metis to turn herself into a fly, and swallowed her. Metis was at the time pregnant with what would have been her first child, who became the goddess Athena. Metis survived inside Zeus' body and set to work making a magical helmet ready for her daughter's birth. This caused Zeus intense pain, so he asked Hephaestus to strike him in the head with an axe.

Whatever the intended outcome of this action, the resulting wound allowed Athena to escape from inside her father. Athena was armoured and ready for war as soon as she was birthed, and joined the gods of Olympus. Metis does not appear to have survived. Some versions of the story of Athena say she was born from Zeus' head and do not mention her mother at all.

BELOW: **A Roman depiction of the birth of Pallas (Athena) from Zeus' head.**

Zeus' second wife was the Titan Themis, who had fought on his side against her kin. She created the natural laws of the universe and the rules that governed proper behaviour, as well as the animals of the land. Their children were the Horae (seasons) and Moirae (fates), all of whom were associated with natural law. Themis resided for a time at Delphi, where she provided oracular prophecy to those who visited, but eventually gifted the oracle to Apollo.

Zeus' third wife was, like Metis, an Oceanid. She was named Eurynome, and may or may not have been the same Titan who lived on Olympus with her husband Ophion until ousted by Chronos. Eurynome bore Zeus three children. These where the Charites, goddesses of grace. Some sources refer to other gods as the father of the Charites, or add additional goddesses to their number.

Zeus and Hera

Zeus' most famous wife was Hera, eldest of the daughters of Chronos and Rhea, and Zeus' sister. Hera appears to be a very ancient goddess, worshipped under various names before the Ancient Greeks began to venerate the Olympian pantheon. Hera is generally depicted as a mature woman and is associated with the family and home. Despite her aspect as a mother-goddess, she is said in some legends to have renewed her virginity annually by bathing in a sacred stream.

ABOVE: Hera is the best known of Zeus' wives; it is widely assumed that she was the only one. In this depiction, a winged goddess – Iris or Hebe – is nearby ready to carry messages on behalf of the Olympian rulers.

Having decided he wanted Hera for his wife, Zeus went about the courtship in a distinctly underhand manner. He transformed himself into a cuckoo, one of the animals with which Hera was associated, and pretended to be injured. Once the goddess was holding the bird to her breast he changed himself back. This rather odd gambit worked. However, the marriage of Hera and Zeus was characterized by infidelity, deception and disputes that often ended up having unpleasant consequences for others. In particular, Hera

HERA'S CHILDREN

Hera had four children by Zeus: Ares, Eileithyia, Hebe and Hephaestus. Hephaestus is sometimes said to have been born without a father, as Hera's way of getting back at Zeus for his many affairs. In one version of the tale, Hephaestus was lame from birth; in others he was injured when Zeus threw him off the mountainside for intervening in one of the couple's many quarrels. Hephaestus was rescued by Thetis and possibly Eurynome, and eventually found a place among the Olympians as the god of fire and metalworking.

was vengeful towards the children of Zeus' lovers as well as the various mortals, nymphs and goddesses themselves.

According to some sources, Hera had an affair with Endymion, who was either a shepherd or a king – sources vary on this point – and extremely handsome. In one variant of the tale, Endymion was cursed by Zeus to sleep eternally. An alternate version has his slumber as a blessing bestowed at the request of Selene, goddess of the moon, so that her mortal lover could remain beautiful forever.

Hera had much to be angry with her husband about. He had many children by various mothers: Apollo and Artemis with the Titan Leto; Hermes with the nymph Maia, and Dionysus with

LEFT: Some tales state that the mortal Endymion was cursed to sleep forever by a vengeful Zeus, others that this was a blessing to enable him to remain forever youthful for his divine lover Selene.

the mortal Semele. Semele met a bad end as a result of Hera's jealousy; she tricked Zeus into allowing Semele to see his true form. Mortals could not look upon a god without expiring, which left the unborn Dionysus motherless. Zeus carried the baby in his thigh until it was time for him to be born.

Zeus produced many children, some of them gods or goddesses and some demigods fathered upon mortals. Hera conspired against many of them, notably the hero Heracles. Not only was Heracles the product of one of Zeus' many infidelities, but Hera was tricked into suckling him as a babe when Athena presented the infant Heracles to her. Heracles was already possessed of superhuman strength, and hurt Hera, causing her milk to splash the sky. This is the legendary origin of the Milky Way.

Hera realized there was something special about this baby when she sent two enormous serpents into his crib. Heracles strangled them and then played with the corpses. Eventually realizing that this was one of her husband's semi-divine children, Hera conspired against Heracles all of his life, to his very great misfortune.

The Gigantomachy

Whether or not some of the Gigantes fought against the Olympians during their war with the Titans, the Gigantomachy was a separate and later conflict. It began with the theft of cattle from Helios by the giant Alcyoneus and escalated rapidly into all-out conflict. Zeus was aware that he needed a mortal on his side to win, but so was Gaea, who had instigated the conflict.

Gaea sought a herb to make her giants invulnerable to the blows of Zeus' mortal champion, but was forestalled by Zeus. At his request, Eos, Helios and Selene halted in their normal movements, depriving the world of light while Zeus gathered all the plants that Gaea might find useful. Despite this prudent action, Alcyoneus was still a formidable foe. He is described as being as big as a mountain and capable of hurling rocks that could slaughter several heroes at once. Heracles countered this advantage by using arrows dipped in the toxic blood of the Hydra. With

BELOW: A bronze statuette of the infant Hercules (the Roman equivalent of Heracles) strangling the serpents sent by Hera to kill him. The enmity between Heracles and Hera featured in many of his adventures.

LEFT: Heracles is depicted here as a cunning and skilful warrior, rendering the giant Alcyoneus helpless by pinning his knee and pulling back on his hair before delivering the fatal blow.

these he dealt Alcyoneus what should have been a mortal wound, but the giant could not be slain on his homeland's soil. No sooner had he fallen than he began to recover, but Athena suggested a solution. Heracles dragged the fallen Alcyoneus out of his homeland to where he could be slain, and finally defeated his foe.

Heracles' battle with Alcyoneus is normally said to have occurred at Phlegra, a peninsula jutting out into the Aegean Sea in Thrace. The area is sometimes called by the more recent name of Pallene; both refer to the same location. Alternative accounts place the battle on the isthmus of Corinth, which joins the Peloponnese to the rest of mainland Greece.

The Gigantomachy was not a straightforward battle but instead appears to have been a drawn-out war of attrition in which the Olympians used a number of clever stratagems to outwit their opponents. Hera was used as bait, distracting the giant Porphyrion with her feminine wiles so that Heracles and Zeus could ambush him with arrows and thunderbolts. Aphrodite took this technique to another level, luring several giants to their doom one by one. Again, it was Heracles who delivered the fatal blows.

BELOW: Heracles encountered the giant Antaeus, who drew power from the earth during his quest for the golden apple. Heracles eventually defeated Antaeus by holding him aloft until his strength drained away.

Some of the gods fought in a more conventional manner; Hermes with his sword and Artemis with her bow. Zeus threw his thunderbolts and Hephaestus used molten metal to slay the giant Mimas. Meanwhile, Poseidon hurled an island (possibly Nisyros or Kos) at Polybotes. Athena fought as a conventional warrior some of the time but used Sicily as her weapon to kill Enceladus.

The only allies the Olympians had were the three Moirae, the Fates, who took a direct approach and beat to death the giants Agrius and Thoas with bronze clubs. By the time the fighting was over, it was obvious that the prophecy had been correct: Heracles had slain more of the Gigantes that anyone else, and had turned the tide of the Gigantomachy. Another half-human demigod, Dionysus, also slew several of the giants.

With the end of the Gigantomachy, the greatest challenge to the reign of the Olympians was over. Threats did emerge, such as the monstrous Typhon, but never again did Olympus face a massed invasion by powerful beings. Now the greatest danger to the Olympians was from within; intrigues, jealousies and feuds that threatened to pit the gods against one another. Indeed, during the war, Hera had tried to get Dionysus killed by manipulating giants into attacking him. Her jealousy over Dionysus' parentage apparently outweighed her loyalty to the Olympian cause. This would not be the last time Hera plotted against one of the illegitimate sons of Zeus.

Poseidon

Some sources portray Poseidon as an aspect of Zeus rather than a separate god. Poseidon seems to have been worshipped, probably under a different name, in very ancient times and morphed into the Greek god of the sea as the myths were retold and rationalized. Some versions of Poseidon's tale say that he was not swallowed by Chronos, but was hidden by his mother in a similar manner to

LEFT: Poseidon is credited with creating Skyphios, the first horse. The association with a land creature may seem odd, but wave crests are often referred to as 'white horses' and Poseidon used horses to pull his chariot.

Zeus. In this version of the tale, Poseidon was hidden among a flock of lambs in Arcadia.

In the commonly accepted legend of Poseidon, he received his trident from the Cyclopes, who made it as one of the godly weapons intended to defeat the Titans. However, there is an alternate version in which Poseidon was sent to be raised on the island of Rhodes by the Telchines. The origins of the Telchines vary from one tale to another; they may have been children of Pontus and Gaea, or of another pair of powerful beings. Blood from the castration of Uranus is another suggested origin.

The Telchines were skilled metalworkers who made Poseidon's trident, and had magical powers including the ability to change their shape and to cause storms. The end of the Telchines is as ambiguous as their origin. They turned their powers to evil and were destroyed by Poseidon (or possibly Zeus or Apollo, depending on the version of the tale).

Like many of the Greek gods, Poseidon is depicted as riding in a four-horse chariot much of the time, and is armed with a trident. Poseidon used this weapon, banging it against a rock, to create the first horse, who was named Skyphios. This is not the only association

POSEIDON AND THE PATRONAGE OF ATHENS

Poseidon was subordinate to Zeus, but he was proud and wilful. He took part in Hera's rebellion against Zeus and was savagely punished for it. He was also at odds with other gods from time to time. At one point, Poseidon decided that the city of Athens should transfer its allegiance from Athena to him, as it would benefit greatly from his patronage. There was some sense in this: Athens was a major maritime power and would indeed find advantage in Poseidon's support.

To demonstrate his point, Poseidon created a stream of seawater originating at the Acropolis. Athena countered this by creating an olive tree, which the king of Athens, Cecrops, decided was more beneficial to the city. Athena retained the loyalty of the city and the dispute was resolved – apparently amicably, since the olive branch has become a universal symbol of peace and reconciliation.

Poseidon has with horses. The goddess Demeter transformed herself into a mare to escape Poseidon's amorous advances. Undeterred, he turned himself into a stallion and fathered a talking horse named Arion and a nymph named Despoena.

Poseidon had many affairs and possibly hundreds of children, but he does not appear to have been particularly attractive as a partner. His eventual wife, Amphitrite, fled to the Atlas Mountains to escape him and was only talked into returning by Delphinus, who was rewarded with the creation of a constellation in his image. Amphitrite bore Poseidon three children: Triton, Rhode and Benthesikyme.

RIGHT: Despite serious misgivings at first, Amphitrite married Poseidon and bore him three children. He had many more by different mothers, not always consensually. Ancient Greek writers do not seem to have found this reprehensible.

Some versions of the story give Rhode different origins, but most agree that she was the personification of the island of Rhodes. Until her birth the island did not exist, but rose from the waters, which solved a problem for the gods. Helios, busy flying across the sky in his chariot, had missed out on a division of territories on the earth. Now, with the agreement of Zeus, he took Rhode to be his wife and became associated with the island.

Few of Poseidon's affairs seem to have turned out this well. He pursued many women, and those he could not win over were taken by force or tricked into relations with him. This was the downfall of the mortal Medusa, who was a famous beauty until

being cursed by Athena for allowing Poseidon to father children upon her. These were born after Medusa was killed by the demigod Perseus. One was a powerful warrior named Chrysaor, who played little part in further events; the other was the winged horse Pegasus.

Poseidon was also the father of the semi-divine hero Theseus, and the enemy of Odysseus. Frequently at odds with Zeus, he was once punished (along with Apollo) by being forced to build fortifications for the Trojan king Laomedon. He was promised payment for this task, but the Trojan king rather unwisely went back on his word. Poseidon took the Greek side in the Trojan wars, to Zeus' further displeasure.

Hades

Hades, brother of Zeus and Poseidon, received the underworld as his domain after the Titanomachy. This gave him power over the dead, and since all living things – plants and animals as well as people – eventually came to his halls, Hades had an association with plenty and riches.

Hades' realm was known by his name, or sometimes as the House of Hades. This can cause confusion as to whether Hades was a place or a god. Anyone who 'went to Hades' encountered both, as they were judged by the god before entering the land of the same name. Hades was fair but pitiless, impossible to bribe or sway with lamentations or flattery.

ABOVE: Hades' abduction of Persephone might have been entirely successful but for the intervention of Hecate and Helios. Persephone's mother Demeter defied Zeus and held the world to ransom in order to get her daughter back.

BELOW: **The return of Persephone was bittersweet. She was freed from Hades, but only for part of the year. During the other months, Demeter's curse lay over the world, bringing the desolation of winter.**

Hades' unswerving nature made him a stern master, but it was not entirely a negative trait. He may have gained his wife through trickery and deceit but at least he was faithful to her. Hades' wife was Persephone, daughter of Zeus and Demeter. When Hades became infatuated with Persephone, he asked Zeus' permission to take her as his wife. Zeus agreed, without consulting either Persephone or her mother.

Hades used a magical flower to trap Persephone, who innocently went to pick the magical blossom. As soon as she touched it, Hades carried her off in his chariot and hid her away in the underworld. Persephone cried out for help but was heard only by Hecate and Helios. Neither acted, probably because they were unsure of what had happened.

When Demeter found her daughter missing, she began to search and was told by Hecate that a cry had been heard. Hecate had not seen the incident and did not know what had happened, but Helios might have done as he saw all things from his place in the heavens. Helios did indeed know that Zeus and Hades had conspired to carry off Persephone, but advised Demeter not to interfere. Hades was powerful and wealthy, and might actually prove to be a good husband. He was certainly not a desirable enemy, and he had the backing of Zeus in the matter.

The wrath of Demeter
Demeter would have none of it. She cursed the world with barrenness, stopping all harvests and the production of food. Ultimately this would kill all mortals, but Demeter was resolute. She ignored the entreaties of other gods to relent and carried on starving the world until Hades finally agreed to release his bride. However, he had tricked Persephone into eating a pomegranate seed while in Hades, which bound her there.

A compromise was agreed, in which Persephone would spend a third of the year in Hades with her husband, and the remainder with her mother in the surface world. During her time in Hades, she is described as fearsome and angry, while on the surface she was happy. For her part, Demeter released the world from her curse, but only while Persephone was outside Hades. Once her daughter went back to the grim realm of the dead, harsh winter gripped the surface world and made life a struggle for its inhabitants.

This incident sheds much light on the character of the Greek gods. Zeus was willing to give away his daughter without even consulting her, while Demeter and Hades were unconcerned that their dispute would bring great suffering and eventual annihilation upon mortals. Zeus was mostly concerned that the death of all mortals would mean no more sacrifices in his honour. As usual, the squabbles of the gods wrought suffering in the mortal world, and none of the gods seem to have cared much.

The Afterlife and the Underworld

The Ancient Greek perception of the afterlife evolved over time. Early accounts state that the realm of Hades was a grim and dreary place, and that very few mortals were permitted to reach the much more pleasant land of Elysium. Later, it seems that the fate of mortals was more varied and that entrance into Elysium required less notable deeds. It was still necessary to live a good life to get into Elysium, caring about others and taking actions for reasons other than pleasure or self-interest.

The Myth of Er

The most coherent account of the fate of the dead is the Myth of Er, recounted in the works of Plato. Er, a warrior who was slain in battle, returned to life to describe the process of judgement and reincarnation. Er was first taken to a palace that had two doors leading to the sky and two to the earth. The dead were judged and told whether to fly through the sky to their next destination or to take the arduous and painful route through the earth.

Both routes led to the same destination, although some of those sent through the earth remained there. These were serious criminals and those judged unworthy of being reincarnated. They followed the same path as the other souls trudging through the torments of the underground path, but just as

THE HOUND OF HADES

Many accounts of the afterlife mention Kerberos, a three-headed hound owned by Hades. 'Hound' in this case does not necessarily mean a dog-like creature, though this is the common interpretation. 'Hound' essentially means a faithful creature that can pursue fugitives and guard the entrance. Hades had other hounds who were spirits rather than dogs, and Kerberos is sometimes depicted in other forms.

Kerberos apparently greeted new arrivals in a friendly fashion but would not allow anyone to leave without Hades' permission. This was rarely granted, although there are stories of great heroes and demigods who returned from Hades with the agreement of its ruler.

BELOW: **Kerberos is most commonly depicted as a three-headed dog.**

they were to be released they were carried off to further punishment and ultimately sent to the pit of Tartarus.

The rest who took the earthly route suffered along the way, as punishment for their bad deeds in their previous life, but eventually emerged to greet those who had flown through the sky. The journey took a 1000 years – 10 times the assumed span of a human life – and each wrong done was punished 10 times in that period. Meanwhile, those who had lived a good life had a much easier journey in which they were rewarded 10 times for each good deed or act of kindness. However, this was not necessarily to their advantage.

The dead were then brought before the throne of Ananke, a primordial goddess representing inevitability or 'necessity' (the terms means the same thing in this legend). Souls requested how their next life would be, and Ananke decided how this was to play out. Er observed that those who had been punished by having to go through the earth made better choices than those who had flown through the sky, perhaps due to a clearer perception of consequences.

Once their next life was decided upon, mortals were taken to the river Lethe. Drinking from the river caused them to forget their previous lives and readied souls to be reborn into the mortal world. Not all of them chose to be reborn as humans. Er witnessed several notable figures, including Agamemnon and

ABOVE: According to the Myth of Er, the spindle of Ananke stood at the centre of the world, with the heavens revolving around it. The concept of a cosmic spindle does not appear in all versions of Ancient Greek cosmology.

Ajax, selecting to return as animals as a result of the sufferings they had endured as humans. Odysseus chose to return as a common man without large concerns, having had enough of great deeds and grand responsibilities. Animals also went through the same process. Some chose to return as different species; some as humans.

During his travels in the underworld Er witnessed the Spire of Necessity, around which the cosmos revolved. The spire acted as a spindle upon which the spheres of the heavens could rotate, except for the outermost, which was fixed in place. This held the stars, with each inner sphere revolving separately and the others carrying the sun and planets as they revolved. The three Fates occasionally assisted the revolution of the cosmos, each associated with one or more of the planets.

When he had seen the process all the way through, Er was sent back to his own body with his memories intact, awakening on his funeral pyre to carry the tale back to the land of the living. It is notable that Plato, who was greatly concerned with making philosophical points by way of stories, relates this legend. Plato's point seems to be that nobody's life is perfect and everyone would choose to swap with someone else rather than live the same life again. The legend of Er reminds the listener that it is important to act out of more than just self-interest and to properly respect the gods. Thus, it is not certain whether this legend reflects the prevailing beliefs of the time or was invented by Plato in order to push his philosophical agenda.

The notion of reincarnation

The idea of reincarnation does not appear much outside Plato's work. The conventional view in the time of Homer (around 700BC) was that the dead wandered forever in a dreary wasteland, and in some cases they are described as becoming little more than unrecognizable skeletons. In later centuries, this view was modified, and people who lived a good life could expect to enter Elysium, providing their good deeds in the mortal world were remembered.

The duty to remember the dead kindly was part of a concept called 'Eusebia', which can best be described as the social and divine responsibilities of a mortal. This included veneration of the gods and acting in a manner that benefited society as a whole, but also extended to ensuring that the departed were fondly remembered even if they were not paragons of virtue in life. In Ancient Greece, a person had a social responsibility not to speak ill of the dead.

Those who did not leave behind an impression in the memory of other mortals were forever condemned to wander Hades in much the same way as Homer's version. Those who were evil were sent to Tartarus, far below and much worse than the relatively mild realm of Hades. Thus, it was the memory of the living that to a great extent decided the fate of the dead.

Aphrodite

The commonly accepted origin of Aphrodite holds that Uranus' blood fell into the sea when he was castrated by Chronos, and from it came Aphrodite. Other versions claim that she was a daughter of Zeus and the Oceanid Dione. Some sources make

BELOW: The marriage of the lame Hephaestus to Aphrodite may have been a shrewd move on the part of Zeus, who knew the value of the weapons and devices a loyal forge-god would produce.

Dione a wife of Zeus – possibly his first – whereas in others she is a daughter of Atlas and not the mother of Aphrodite.

Aphrodite was associated with beauty and desire, and not surprisingly had many lovers. Among them were Ares and Hermes, with whom she had children, and Adonis, who she had to share with Persephone. Although Aphrodite could be seen as the antithesis of war, she played an important part in the Gigantomachy, luring giant warriors into an ambush, and she fought for Troy in the Trojan War. However, when Typhon attacked Olympus, Aphrodite prudently hid from the monster by turning herself into a fish.

Aphrodite was involved in the incident that started the Trojan War, and the Olympian gods feared she might cause conflict among them with her beauty and allure. Zeus decided to forestall this possibility by marrying Aphrodite to Hephaestus, who was both unattractive and fearsome.

Among Aphrodite's children was Eros, a minor god with the same name as one of the primordial deities. Eros accompanied Aphrodite wherever she went, inciting passion in whomever he shot with magical arrows made by Hephaestus.

BELOW: When Perseus slew the gorgon Medusa, Hephaestus mounted her head on the magical shield Aegis, which was already perhaps his greatest creation. Aegis was borne by both Zeus and Athena at times.

Hephaestus

Hephaestus was the child of Hera, with or without the assistance of Zeus depending on the legend. He was not an attractive child, and was lamed when he was thrown off Mount Olympus by either Zeus or Hera. Despite his deformity – which was highly unusual among the physically perfect gods – he was rescued by Thetis and Eurynome and hidden away from his parents.

Hephaestus returned to Olympus and was recognized as a master craftsman, enabling him to take revenge on Hera. Hephaestus fashioned a golden throne that pleased his mother – at least until she sat upon it. Then, she found herself entangled in fine golden cords that none but Hephaestus could see.

He refused all entreaties to release Hera until Dionysus bribed him with drink and the other gods granted him a place on Olympus.

Once installed in Olympus, Hephaestus set about making magical devices for gods and heroes in his forge. Not all of these creations were beneficial to the gods, however. Hephaestus made a magical chain net to snare Ares and Aphrodite during one of their trysts, exposing their affair to the other gods. Hephaestus seems to have favoured Eros, one of the children of Ares and Aphrodite, and made magical arrows for him. Harmonia, another of their children, was given a magical necklace that brought bad luck on her and those who owned it thereafter.

ABOVE: The Titan Leto, mother of Apollo and Artemis, was beset by serpents and forced to flee. Her lover Zeus gave her no help at all, but her twin children turned out to be formidable allies.

Most of Hephaestus' works were helpful to their owners, however. The sword of Peleus and the shield of Achilles were among his creations, as were Agamemnon's sceptre and Athena's shield Aegis. Hephaestus had assistance in his endeavours, from the mighty Cyclopes and from automatons that he built for himself. He also constructed the palaces of the gods in Olympus.

Apollo and Artemis

Apollo and Artemis were twins, fathered upon the Titan Leto by Zeus. Hera found out about the liaison and arranged for Leto to be harried across the land. In some versions of the tale, Hera sent one or more monstrous dragons or serpents, children of Gaea, to pursue Leto; in others, the serpents performed the same role but of their own accord. Sources vary on the identity of the serpents. Some say the serpent was a dragon named Delphyne, who was normally charged with protecting the oracle at Delphi. Others say it was Python, or both Python and Delphyne.

Leto eventually came the island of Delos, which was not connected to the seabed and was thus technically not 'land'. There, she gave birth to Artemis but was too exhausted to birth her second child. She was assisted by the infant Artemis, who

BELOW: Apollo was the greatest musician in the universe, and he had the godly powers to prove it. Anyone he could not out-play he defeated in rigged contests, often taking horrible vengeance on those who dared challenge him.

acted as midwife to her twin Apollo. Zeus gifted the two baby gods with bows, which were soon put to good use. At only four days old, Apollo shot and killed one of the pursuing serpents, although this brought new problems. Gaea was angered at the death of her child and ordained that Apollo must serve King Admetus of Pherae for a year as penance.

Apollo and his associations

Apollo presumably matured fast, for by the end of his servitude he was a friend of King Admetus and capable of performing godly deeds. He helped Admetus win the hand of Alcestis, daughter of Pelias, who would one day organize the first Olympic Games. Apollo clearly thought highly of his former master, and assured him that when Admetus' time came to die he would be allowed to live on providing someone else took his place. In due course, the time came and Alcestis took his place in the underworld. She was later returned to her husband by Heracles.

Apollo was associated with light and reason and also with music and art. He was at times prone to be vengeful, especially when he felt his supremacy as a musician was challenged. He traded magical cattle and a golden wand to Hermes for the lyre and pan-pipes, and naturally believed he was the greatest musician in the cosmos. When Pan contested against Apollo with the pan-pipes, most of the judges ruled in favour of Apollo, but King Midas preferred Pan's music. Apollo gave King Midas donkey ears as a punishment.

Apollo was much harsher with Marsyas, a satyr who thought he was a better musician than Apollo. Determined to win their contest, Apollo insisted that they play their instruments upside down. This was possible with Apollo's lyre but not with Marsyas' flute, so the satyr lost. Apollo had him tied to a tree and flayed alive, after which he was turned into a stream.

Cinyras, king of Cyprus, also met a bad end as a result of challenging Apollo to a musical contest, although sources do not agree as to whether he killed himself or was slain by Apollo.

LEFT: It is not clear exactly what about Zeus' seduction of Callisto angered Artemis the most; the nymph's lack of faith to her chaste sisterhood, or the fact that Zeus took the form of Artemis carry out the seduction.

Artemis and her associations

Artemis could also be unnecessarily wrathful. Niobe, daughter of Tantalus and queen of Thebes, decided that she was superior to Leto as Niobe had seven daughters and seven sons, and Leto had only one of each. Apollo and Artemis responded by murdering all of Niobe's children with their bows. Some versions have Apollo carrying out the massacre alone; others have Artemis killing all the female children and Apollo the males.

Artemis was sometimes referred to as Delia, after the island of her birth. She was associated with the hunt and with a quick, painless death. The two went well together; hunters would not

ABOVE: In one version of the tale Artemis was tricked into slaying her lover Orion by a jealous Apollo. This does not seem to have unduly strained the twin gods' relationship.

want to see prey suffer unnecessarily, even if only out of self-interest. A wounded animal might run far enough to be lost, whereas one that was dispatched by a well-placed arrow would be easy to find. However, Artemis was not above causing suffering when she saw fit; the hunter Acteon saw her naked while she was bathing, so she turned him into a stag and let his dogs do the rest.

Nor was Artemis particularly fair in her judgements of others. She kept the company of a group of nymphs, all of whom were as chaste as Artemis. Zeus disguised himself as Artemis in order to seduce one of their number, Callisto, and she became pregnant. Artemis became suspicious when Callisto would not undress to bathe, so the other nymphs forced her. Once Callisto's pregnancy was revealed, Artemis turned her into a bear for breaking her vow of chastity.

Like her brother Apollo, Artemis was proud. When King Agamemnon boasted that his hunting skills were superior to hers, Artemis trapped Agamemnon's fleet – due to sail for Troy to take part in the siege there – in harbour with adverse winds. Artemis demanded the sacrifice of Agamemnon's daughter Iphigenia, although she eventually accepted a deer in the girl's place. Iphigenia became a priestess of Artemis instead, possibly out of gratitude that seems a little misplaced.

Others encountered Artemis' vengeful side, such as the hunter Orion. According to one story, Orion mistreated a member of Artemis' band of nymphs, possibly Artemis herself. The goddess sent a scorpion to kill Orion, and both subsequently became constellations in the night sky. An alternative version of the death of Orion states that he and Artemis were in love, and Apollo was jealous of anyone taking his sister's attention away from him. When Orion was swimming and his head was visible only as a small object above the water, Apollo bet Artemis that she could not hit such a small target. Not knowing what it was but quite able to hit it, Artemis duly put an arrow in Orion's head.

Apollo's lovers

Apollo had many lovers. Some affairs seem to have turned out reasonably well, but many did not. This was largely the result of the same jealousy that resulted in Orion's death. When Apollo's lover Coronis fell in love with a mortal named Ischys, a crow told him about it. Crows were at the time white, but Apollo burned it black in his rage. Coronis was slain by Artemis, although her baby survived. He was Asclepius, and would eventually be the god of medicine.

Cassandra was gifted with the power of prophecy by Apollo in an effort to win her over, but she resisted his advances. Unable to take back the gift, Apollo instead cursed Cassandra to be unable to persuade anyone that she was telling the truth. She was thus forced to endure being able to tell the future without the ability to do anything about it.

BELOW: Although Apollo was beautiful, wise and surely the greatest of all musicians, there were those who resisted his charms. Among them was Daphne, who asked to be turned into a laurel tree to escape Apollo's advances.

Some of Apollo's lovers ended up as trees or other plants. The nymph Daphne wanted to remain chaste and asked to be transformed in order to resist Apollo's advances. She was turned into a laurel tree, and Apollo wore a laurel wreath thereafter as a reminder of her. His male lover Cyparissus, heartbroken over accidentally killing a pet deer that Apollo had given him, asked to have his sorrow made permanent and was turned into a cypress tree.

Hyacinthus was also a victim of jealousy, but not Apollo's. Zephyrus, god of the west wind, is normally considered the most gentle of winds, but he loved Hyacinthus and could not bear to see him with Apollo. Zephyrus blew Hyacinthus' discus back at him, inflicting a mortal wound. Apollo saved his lover from the realm of Hades by turning him into a flower.

Apollo is generally venerated as a highly positive god, associated with music and reason – hallmarks of civilization. Artemis is a skilled, honourable and chaste huntress. Yet both were capable of murderous actions inspired by a jealousy that could be described as being rather petty.

Ares

Ares was venerated as the Greek god of war, although he might better be considered to personify violence than organized warfare. He was the son of Zeus and Hera, and thus one of the legitimate children of the king of the gods. Despite this, Ares played a fairly small part in the mythology of Olympus, often as an opponent for wiser or smarter gods. It is possible to find a metaphor here for the triumph of reason over blind rage and the rise of civilization from barbarism, but it is equally possible that clever gods simply had more interesting stories than someone who responded to any situation with homicidal rage.

Ares had many lovers, notably Aphrodite. He was caught by her husband Hephaestus in a trap of golden cords and ridiculed by the other gods, but still managed to father several children upon her. These included Harmonia, goddess of harmony, and – according to some versions – Eros. Phobos (fear) and Deimos (terror) were also children of Ares and Aphrodite, and later accompanied their father in his travels and his many fights.

ARES AND ADONIS

Ares was jealous of Aphrodite's affections even though he was not her husband. When she fell in love with the mortal Adonis, Ares murdered him. Adonis was a mortal of unusual parentage as a result of Aphrodite's jealousy. Offended by the beauty of Myrrha, daughter of King Cinyrus of Cyprus, Aphrodite took revenge by causing Cinyrus to father a child – Adonis – upon her. When he found out what had happened, Cinyrus decided to kill his daughter and their unborn child, but Aphrodite saved the girl by turning her into a myrrh tree.

In one version of the story, Aphrodite gave the unborn Adonis to Persephone to look after, and Persephone was so taken by his beauty that she would not give him back. Zeus eventually decreed that Adonis must spend half his time with each, creating a variant on the theme that winter and summer were the result of someone living part of the year in the underworld. In this case, it was Adonis rather than Persephone that caused the change of seasons.

In another version of the tale, Aphrodite pursued Adonis, who was intent upon hunting and not interested in a relationship. Aphrodite begged Adonis not to risk his life hunting, but he would not listen. Ares, jealous despite the fact that Adonis had turned Aphrodite down, turned himself into a ferocious wild boar and confronted Adonis, goring him mortally. Aphrodite was able to reach Adonis in time to turn his blood droplets into anemones, but the beautiful youth was dead. In this version of the tale, Zeus allowed Adonis to return from the underworld for half the year.

BELOW: **Ares murdered Adonis despite the fact that he was not interested in a relationship with Aphrodite – who was another god's wife in any case.**

ABOVE: Athena and Ares met in battle at the siege of Troy, where Athena defeated Ares and drove him from the field. This may be a metaphor for the triumph of organized warfare over simple savagery.

Ares had numerous mortal children, including King Tereus of Thrace, who was a thoroughly bad character. After forcing himself upon his wife's sister Philomena he imprisoned her and cut out her tongue. Philomena revealed the deed by clever embroidery, at which point Tereus carried on the family tradition by trying to kill his wife and her sister. All three were then turned into birds by the gods; Tereus into a predatory hawk and the women into a nightingale and a swallow.

Ares was also the father of the Amazons, a fierce tribe of female warriors who were involved in the Trojan Wars and found themselves at odds with the heroes Heracles and Theseus on other occasions. Ares himself took part in the Trojan Wars. He promised Hera and Athena that he would join the Greek side, but was persuaded by Aphrodite to transfer his support to the Trojans.

At first this went well for the Trojan side, but after the hero Diomedes had wounded Aphrodite and driven her from the field Athena herself assisted him against Ares. Athena deflected Ares' mighty spear thrust and guided Diomedes' own weapon, adding godly strength to a blow that seriously wounded Ares. This incident may be a metaphor for the triumph of organization and generalship (represented by Athena) over the brute violence of the warrior. Whatever the case, Ares was defeated by Athena and fled the field of battle.

Athena

Athena was the child of Zeus and his first wife Metis, although the manner of her birth was such that Zeus is sometimes credited with creating the goddess alone. He swallowed his pregnant wife, presumably killing her as she does not appear in later myths, but the baby Athena continued to grow inside Zeus. She was eventually born from his head, fully grown and armed for war.

Athena represented wisdom and learning as well as skilled crafts such as spinning and weaving. As a warrior, she was wise and cunning where Ares was just violent, and thus represented generalship and military organization; she was a goddess of generals and soldiers rather than warriors. She was closely associated with the city of Athens, winning a contest with Poseidon to be its patron. Athena's gift of an olive tree was deemed more useful than Poseidon's gift of a seawater stream, and she retained the loyalty of the city.

Athena was chaste, although she was desired by many. Among them was Hephaestus, who attempted to rape her. Perhaps surprisingly, the forge-god did not meet a violent end at Athena's hands, although he was unsuccessful in his attempt. His seed fell upon the ground, impregnating Gaea, who produced a son named Erikthonios. Athena raised the boy as her own child.

Athena was involved in the incident that started the Trojan War, whereby Eris, goddess of discord, gatecrashed the wedding of Thetis and Peleus. Eris had

BELOW: Athena is normally depicted as a wise and noble warrior. She was not, usually, prone to the same spite and jealousy as many other gods, but she did compete with Hera and Aphrodite during the Judgement of Paris.

not been invited as she was a troublemaker, but took revenge by throwing a golden apple into the festivities to be claimed by the fairest of the goddesses. This provoked jealousy and infighting as Hera, Aphrodite and Athena all tried to claim it. Zeus was asked to decide who was the fairest and should therefore have the apple, but perhaps wisely handed the task off to Paris of Troy.

The three goddesses tried to bribe Paris, who decided that Aphrodite's offer was the best. This was the ability to seduce Helen, wife of King Menelaus of Troy. The Judgement of Paris, as the incident was known, is generally considered the trigger incident for the Trojan Wars; Paris' abduction of Helen sparked a campaign to return her in which Athena fought on the Greek side.

Athena was a patroness to heroes, including Heracles, Perseus and Odysseus. She was sometimes the bearer of the Aegis, which is variously described as a shield or a breastplate. It is sometimes depicted as bearing the head of Medusa the gorgon, who was slain by Perseus.

BELOW: Dishonest as well as vain, Hera, Aphrodite and Athena immediately resorted to bribery when Paris was asked to decide which of them was the fairest. Athena, at least, might have known better than to get involved in such a petty contest.

Demeter

Demeter was the goddess of harvests, often depicted with a cornucopia, or horn of plenty. One of the original Olympians, Demeter was a daughter of Chronos and Rhea, and was associated with natural laws as well as the bounty of the earth. Demeter was for the most part a generous goddess, but could be violent at times. She is described as fighting against the Gigantes with a golden sword during the Gigantomachy, and she cursed the world with famine when her daughter Persephone was abducted by Hades.

During her wanderings in search of her missing daughter, Demeter was befriended by the household of King Keleos and Queen Metaneira, who recognized her as someone important despite her disguise as an old woman. The queen had borne a child at quite an advanced age and was concerned about her ability to care for it properly. She asked Demeter to look after the baby, who was named Demophoon. Demeter did so, feeding him ambrosia, the food of the gods.

Demeter hoped to give the baby divine powers, but Queen Metaneira did not understand what Demeter was doing when she hid her infant son in the fire at night. Metaneira was naturally concerned for his safety, but her interference angered Demeter, who had intended for the boy to be immortal and unageing. In some versions of the tale, Demophoon was killed by the fire; in others he grew up like an immortal, but did not achieve the potential Demeter had seen in him. She did reveal her godly status to Metaneira, and instructed her to build a temple where Demeter brooded and grieved for her missing daughter. When Persephone was released from Hades – albeit for only part of the year – Demeter finally lifted her curse and allowed food to be grown once again.

Hermes

Hermes was the child of Zeus and the nymph Maia, daughter of Atlas. He was adventurous and athletic from the moment he was born, sneaking out as his mother slept to steal the cattle of Apollo. Wisely sacrificing two of the stolen cattle to the gods, he then made a lyre out of a tortoise that he had killed and learned to play it.

BELOW: Demeter was in general a positive and nurturing goddess, who fed the world with her bounty. When angered, however, she could be as vicious as any other Olympian, and was not averse to wiping out all mortal life if need be.

Apollo tracked down his missing cattle and accused Hermes of stealing them. The baby was at that point asleep after a busy first morning in the world, and his mother was not inclined to believe he could have done anything in the few hours since his birth. Apollo found the tortoise-lyre, strung with the guts of his cattle, and took this to Zeus as proof.

Zeus told baby Hermes to give back the cattle, but instead Apollo traded them for the lyre. Thus Hermes became a patron of travellers, traders, thieves and herdsmen. He also became associated with athletics and astronomy in addition to his role as messenger. Hermes was not merely a bearer of information; he acted as a guide to the dead, showing them the way to Hades, and at times was given errands to carry out for the other gods.

Hermes had few stories of his own, but featured in many myths about the other gods. Often he was a facilitator or a guide, such as when he led Hera, Athena and Aphrodite to Mount Ida to receive the Judgement of Paris. Hermes carried the infant Dionysus to King Athamas, with instructions from Zeus to raise the child.

BELOW: Hermes' theft of Apollo's cattle proved his worth to Zeus, who often had need of a clever and less-than-honest messenger. He was an adept trader when thievery was not sufficient to get the job done.

LEFT: Chione's fate in many ways sums up the attitude of Olympian gods to mortals. Chione was slain by Artemis in vengeance for somehow managing to find something positive about being raped by two gods in the same night.

He also rescued Io, a lover of Zeus' who had been turned into a cow, from the giant Argus Panoptes. Hermes also interceded on behalf of heroes and arranged deals on behalf of others.

Hermes fathered the god Pan, whose mother may have been a nymph or a mortal depending on the version of the story. Pan was a strange-looking creature, whose own mother fled in fear when she saw him, but when Hermes took him to Olympus he was universally popular. Hermes had other children, although he never formed a permanent partnership with any other gods or goddesses. With Aphrodite he had Hermaphrodites and possibly Tyche, and when Hermes and Apollo both raped Chione in the same night she had a son named Philammon by Apollo and one named Autolycus by Hermes.

The rape of Chione represented gods forcing themselves upon mortals; not an uncommon event in Greek mythology. Hermes used magic to make Chione sleep, while Apollo used deception. Chione herself is represented as being strangely pleased with the situation, boasting that since she had been violated by two gods she must be more beautiful even than Artemis. Hearing of this, Artemis murdered her out of jealousy. Chione's father Daedalion threw himself off a mountainside out of grief, but was saved by Apollo, who turned him into a hawk. This act seems to indicate at least a measure of remorse, which is unusual in Greek myths – mostly the gods do as they please with mortals and are not concerned about any resulting suffering.

Dionysus

Dionysus was one of Zeus' illegitimate children, by a mortal princess named Semele. Hera, not unreasonably, was jealous of Zeus' infidelity and demanded he reveal himself to Semele in all his glory. In some versions of the tale, she was tricked into asking him to prove he was a god. Either way, Semele perished, as all mortals did when looking upon a god – in this case consumed by the power of Zeus' thunderbolts.

Zeus saved the baby and nurtured him within his own thigh, sending him to the nymphs of Mount Nysa to be raised. Later, Dionysus was taken by Hermes to King Athamas, who was married to Semele's sister Ino. This enraged Hera, who drove Athamas mad. Athamas slew one of his children; Ino and their other son Melicertes threw themselves into the sea to escape him.

Dionysus does not appear to have come to harm at this point, but he became associated with madness as well as wine and

BELOW: King Midas showed great hospitality to Dionysus' friend and mentor, the Satyr Silenus. For once, his dire fate was the result of his own bad choices – Dionysus warned him against his chosen reward but felt honour-bound to bestow it.

festivities. He used this power to take revenge on his enemies, driving king Lykourgos of Thrace mad in revenge for attacking Dionysus and his companions. Lykourgos killed his own family, whereas the daughters of King Pentheus of Thebes were caused to rip him apart in a frenzy. Dionysus caused this madness in revenge for failing to recognize he was a god.

Dionysus was not always vengeful or angry. He helped to resolve a confrontation in Olympus by getting Hephaestus drunk, persuading the angry forge-god to release his mother Hera from the golden throne-trap he had created. He often acted as a go-between in dealings with the underworld, and journeyed there in several myths. He was eventually accepted as one of the gods, joining Zeus' ruling council.

In the legend of King Midas, Dionysus offered to reward Midas with anything he wanted in return for assisting Dionysus' old mentor Silenus. Silenus had become drunk and managed to get lost, but was given hospitality by Midas. Although Dionysus advised against Midas' chosen reward – that anything he touched should turn to gold – he was forced to keep his promise. Once Midas realized his mistake – at the cost of his daughter's life and near-starvation – Dionysus showed him how to undo the curse by bathing in the river Pactolus.

Hestia

Hestia was the first child of Chronos and Rhea, and was associated with the hearth and home. Peaceable, wise and disinclined to cause trouble for mortals, she featured in few myths and might be considered the closest thing to a 'good god' among the jealous and sometimes rather nasty Olympians.

Hestia was once the subject of both Apollo and Poseidon's advances, but realized that if she chose one of them the other would cause trouble. Her answer was to swear eternal chastity, for which Zeus rewarded her with great honours and a significant portion of sacrifices made by mortals. She remained in Olympus to tend the hearth fires when the other gods were about their business, and thus played little part in the affairs of the world.

ABOVE: **Dionysus was more than the god of wine; he represented frenzy and inspiration which might or might not be associated with drunkenness. His Roman equivalent Bacchus seems simplistic by comparison.**

3

OTHER GODS AND SPIRITS

The Ancient Greeks had many other gods and semi-divine spirits who did not live on Olympus. Some personified places or aspects of the world, while others were individuals with their own stories.

Many of these gods and spirits were not worshipped as such, but might be encountered by people or heroes going about their business. Some were unfriendly or inimical, and even those who were not hostile to encounter could be dangerous.

Spirits that personified a power or an aspect of the universe were known as daemones. The term 'daemon' or 'demon' did not necessarily have negative connotations. The use of the term in Christian texts, where demons are definitely evil, altered perceptions of the word. Daemones in Ancient Greece all had their own nature and personality, and few if any could be described as simply 'good' or 'evil'. All the same, wise mortals stayed away from them.

OPPOSITE: **The Hesperides, nymphs of the evening, were entrusted with the care of a tree that produced golden apples, which was given to Hera upon her marriage to Zeus. Their garden lay at the western end of the Mediterranean.**

The gods and spirits were often referred to by a variety of names. Sometimes this referred to their place of origin or the region they were associated with. For example, Artemis is sometimes called Delia, in reference to her birth on the island of Delos. Many deities had a number of epithets associated with them, often denoting their different aspects. These might be used in place of their name, creating the impression of a different god. This is particularly confusing if the same epithet was used for more than one deity.

Some gods were worshipped under different names in various places. Artemis was known in Sparta as Artemis Aeginaea, possibly in reference to her prowess with the javelin, and might at times be referred to only by her surname. In some cases, sources seem to refer to one of the primordial gods when they may in fact mean an Olympian or a rustic god, or a spirit whose powers lie in the same realm as those of the primordial god. Thus, a minor sea god might be referred to as Pontus rather than using his actual name, as a sort of general reference to the oceans he was connected with. Some apparently conflicting versions of myths may in fact all refer to the same god or spirit, but by different names and aspects. It is not uncommon for sources to multiply gods into three or more closely associated aspects or much greater numbers of spirits. These are sometimes referred to as offspring, but that does not necessarily mean children as such. They may be essentially small parts of the god broken off to create a retinue of spirits, although over time different writers may have interpreted the concept differently.

Attempts to explain the parentage of these spirits have sometimes resulted in a new myth or an addition to one, wherein the god had a liaison with a nymph, satyr, mortal or another deity. This is one reason why Greek mythology evolved over time; efforts to rationalize stories that by definition lie beyond rational explanation have caused distortions over the centuries.

ABOVE: A Roman depiction of Artemis as goddess of the hunt, dating from around AD200. Artemis was closely associated with many rustic spirits, particularly nymphs of the countryside.

The Erinyes

The Erinyes were created out of the drops of blood that fell from Uranus when he was castrated by Chronos. They are normally depicted as ugly women, winged and with serpents entwined in their hair. Sources are unclear as to how many Erinyes existed. Three are known – Alecto, Megaera and Tisiphone – representing implacable judgement, the bearing of grudges and vengeance itself. Thus it is normally assumed that there were three Erinyes.

The Erinyes brought vengeance and punishment upon those who had committed serious crimes such as oathbreaking, murder and insufficient respect for the gods. Madness was often visited upon those who slew a parent, although disease and starvation were also possibilities. The Erinyes were capable of punishing an individual or a community, such as a city that harboured a fugitive.

Once the wrath of the Erinyes had been called down upon a victim, it was necessary to undergo a ritual atonement, which might take the form of a task or sacrifice. After the intervention of Athena, the Erinyes became less concerned with wrathful vengeance and more interested in justice.

ABOVE: The Erinyes, known to the Romans as Furies, were vengeful spirits who punished wrongdoing. Once the Erinyes were angered the only solution was a ritual purification or absolution, often prescribed by a king or similar authority figure.

The Horae

Ancient Greek mythology includes more than one group of goddesses named the Horae, or Hours. One group represents the three main seasons of the year: Thallo (blossoms), Auxo (growth) and Karpo (harvesting of food). In this aspect, the Horae were also responsible for protecting Olympus by shrouding the way there in clouds. In some versions of the myth these Horae are the children of Aphrodite and Zeus.

It is likely that this was the 'original' version of the Horae, whose work was regulated by natural laws and the general rightness of the universe. This was translated over time into new identities more closely connected with those laws than with the cycles of nature. In this aspect, the three Horae are named Eunomia (good and wise laws), Eirene (peace and prosperity) and Dike (justice). These Horae are sometimes considered to be the children of Zeus and Themis.

These aspects are by no means exclusive. When the natural world progressed correctly according to its laws, mortals experienced times of plenty. Unnatural conditions such as a particularly harsh winter or unseasonal weather brought hard times. The parallel in human society is obvious: peace, harmony and justice led to prosperity, whereas upsets in the natural order of things resulted in the opposite.

Another group of Horae were associated with the twelve hours of the day. An hour was not a fixed length of time in Ancient Greece; it was one-twelfth of the period of daylight. A summer hour was thus longer than a winter one. These Horae

BELOW: **The Horae, like many gods and spirits were represented differently over the long span of Greek mythology. Originally associated with the observable cycles of nature, they came to represent the laws that drove those cycles.**

acted as guides for Helios, scheduling his passage across the daylight sky according to the time available for the journey.

The Moirae

The Moirae are better known as the Fates. Their origins vary from one myth to another; they are sometimes described as being the children of Zeus and Themis, in other places as the offspring of Erebus and Nyx. Plato postulates that they were the children of the primordial goddess Ananke. This origin story makes good mythic sense; the Moirae represented the fate of mortals and descent from the personification of immutable cosmic laws, but Plato was writing later than sources that describe the Moirae as children of gods. He may have been conveniently redefining cosmology to make a point.

The first of the Moirae, Clotho, was responsible for spinning the thread of a person's life. She was not merely a facilitator; she decided on major events and thus had control over the life of a mortal. In some versions of the myth even the gods were subject to Clotho's whim, although in others the thread was spun in accordance with Zeus' wishes.

Lachesis was responsible for measuring the thread of a person's life, and therefore how much time that person was allotted on earth. According to Plato, when that time was up she was involved in the distribution of lots from which a person could choose. This would determine the nature of the person's next life.

ABOVE: Some Ancient Greek sources state that the Moirae, or Fates, decided the events and length of a person's life, while others say that Zeus told them what he wanted for any given mortal.

Atropos wielded the shears that cut the thread of a person's life, bringing it to an end at the time allotted by her sister Lachesis and after the events determined by Clotho. The three Fates thus determined the events of a person's life and the timing of its ending. They might give someone a terrible existence for no discernible reason, and do not seem to have been amenable to persuasion by sacrifice or similar means. However, the Fates were strongly allied to the Olympian gods and fought alongside them when necessary.

Rustic Gods

Many of the Greek deities had a specialized area of interest and were not part of the council of Olympus that decided the great affairs of the universe. Among them were the rustic gods of the countryside. Their activities generally fell under the purview of Artemis, Dionysus or Hermes.

Pan

Best-known of the rustic gods was Pan, the rather strange child of Hermes and a nymph named Penelopeia. Pan is generally depicted as a man with the legs and hindquarters of a goat, along with horns and pointed ears. He lived in Arcadia, where he was the patron of shepherds and herdsmen. Although he watched over those who worked the countryside, he was not above terrorizing them when he felt like it. Pan had the ability to inspire unreasoning and debilitating fear and panic in mortals.

BELOW: Pan was a rather unpredictable deity, who watched over those who worked in the countryside but sometimes terrorized them for no good reason. He is commonly associated with music and lust.

Pan liked to play his pipes and was a musician second only to Apollo – at least he was second according to Apollo, and it was not safe to disagree with him. Pan lusted after many nymphs, not always successfully. One, Syrinx, was turned into a clump of reeds in order to escape him – reeds from which Pan subsequently made his pipes. One version of the tale of Echo has her cursed to fade away, leaving behind only the echo of her voice after refusing Pan's advances. Pan did manage to father a number of children, including some of the goat-footed spirits known as Panes.

Pan was associated with Aristaios, a benevolent god of countryside skills such as beekeeping, hunting and olive-growing as well as the use of medicinal herbs. Aristaios was once a mortal, although accounts of his parentage vary, and was elevated to godhood for his services to humanity. His daughter, the nymph Makris, looked after the infant Dionysus and was punished for it by Hera.

Other rustic gods

Other rustic gods may have been inherited or co-opted from other cultures, but were worshipped in the countryside as patrons of crops, gardens and agriculture. Worship of Attis probably began in Anatolia and spread to Greece, where he was associated with the god Iasion. Iasion was killed by one of Zeus' thunderbolts after a tryst with Demeter. Some sources name him as one half of the constellation Gemini, along with Triptolemos. The latter was a prince who was kind to Demeter while she was mourning the disappearance of Persephone and was rewarded with knowledge of agriculture.

Likewise, the fertility god Priapus was probably adopted by the Greeks from Asia Minor. He was a rather basic fertility god with an enormous penis, largely ignored or derided by scholars and the educated classes but popular in the countryside. Once adopted into Greek mythology, Priapus was given a new backstory as the son of Dionysus, possibly with Aphrodite.

KHEIRON THE CENTAUR

Kheiron, the original centaur, is generally numbered among the rustic gods. Kheiron was the son of the Titan Chronos and possessed great wisdom, he tried to watch over the mortal race of centaurs, and provided advice and teaching to several heroes and gods including Asclepius and Achilles.

Kheiron was eventually wounded by Heracles, who was battling other centaurs and hit Kheiron by mistake. Heracles liked to use hydra venom on his weapons, which inflicted a wound that would never heal and would cause eternal suffering to the immortal Kheiron. He chose to die rather than endure it and was honoured as a constellation.

BELOW: **Kheiron was half-brother to Zeus but much lower status in the cosmic order.**

OPPOSITE: **The fact that Amphitrite, a sea nymph, fled to the dry mountains of North Africa to evade Poseidon suggests that she was very strongly opposed to marrying him. She was won over by Delphinus, a sea-daemon of unknown parentage.**

BELOW: **Triton was originally a single being, whose conch shell trumpet could calm the surface waves. Later sources refer to a class of daemones, like satyrs of the sea, who were both male and female, as Tritons.**

Among the rustic daemones were the Kouretes Daktyloi, who were warrior spirits associated with the island of Crete. Accounts vary as to whether there were three, five or nine of them, but in some versions there were five male Daktyloi who were married to the five female Hekaterides. Their children included the Satyroi and the mortal Kouretes – warrior people of Crete. The Kouretes and their sister-wives the Hekaterides were assigned by Rhea to protect and raise the infant Zeus, concealing his crying from his father Chronos by clashing their weapons and shouting battle cries.

Water Gods

The Ancient Greeks had many gods associated with seas and bodies of water. While Poseidon was the lord of all the seas, these gods were associated with specific bodies of water or aspects of life connected with the seas.

Poseidon and his wife and children

Amphitrite was the eldest of the Nereides (children of Nereus) and thus considered a nymph, but as the wife of Poseidon she was also a god. Although she was at first reluctant to become Poseidon's wife – she fled and hid in the Atlas Mountains to avoid him – she became the mother of fish and sea-creatures. Their children included Benthesikyme, the nymph or goddess associated with deep-water waves, and Kidopolis, the goddess of storm waves who married Briareos. The latter was one of the Hecatoncheires, who afterwards lived with her beneath the sea and made storms. In this guise he was often known as Aigaios, though some sources consider Aigaios to be a separate being.

Poseidon and Amphitrite had two other children: Rhode and Triton. Rhode was the patroness of the island of that name, and married Helios. Triton acted as a herald for his father and carried a conch shell with which he could cause the waves to become calm.

RIGHT: **The Nereids are often depicted as riding on the backs of Hippokampoi, fish-tailed horses, or large fish-like creatures. Each Nereid was associated with an aspect of the sea such as foaming breakers or small waves.**

He was often accompanied by spirits called Tritones. These are sometimes described as his offspring but may have been a sort of godly retinue made up of fragments of Triton himself.

Other sea gods
Not all of the sea gods were descended from Poseidon. Some were left over from the age of the Titans or were the children of primordial gods. Among those was Nereus, often called the Old Man of the Sea. He was a son of Pontus and Gaea, primordial gods of land and sea, and made his home in the Aegean. This made him an important god to the ancient Greeks, who conducted a great deal of sea trade and fishing around the islands of his sea. Indeed, Nereus was closely associated with fishing and the bounty of the sea. Nereus' wife was the Oceanid Doris, and together they had 50 daughters collectively named the Nereids.

In some sources, Glaucus is stated to be a son of Nereus. In others, he is a descendant of Poseidon or one of the other gods. Glaucus became a deity after eating a magic herb planted by the Titan Chronos, and was a benefactor of mariners and fishermen. He visited the shores of Greek lands to make prophecies, which were regarded as extremely reliable. Some sources say he lived on Delos and was associated with the oracle there.

Phorcys, also sometimes referred to as the 'old man of the sea', was another child of Pontus and Gaea. With his wife Keto he ruled over the most dangerous creatures of the oceans. Their children included the Graeae, three strange women who passed their one eye and one tooth back and forth among themselves and guarded the secret location of the cave where dwelt more of Phorcys' children, the Gorgons.

Phorcys was also father to unique monsters such as Skylla and a hundred-headed sea serpent named Ladon, as well as a dragon named Echidna and the nymph Thoosa, who may have been the mother of the Cyclops Polyphemus.

In some myths, Polyphemus attempted to win over the Nereid Galatea, who was associated with calm seas. Despite his gifts and music, Polyphemus was not successful, and flew into a rage when Galatea favoured a mortal named Akis. Polyphemus slew Akis with a boulder, so the gods turned him into a stream that flowed down from Mount Etna; he became its god.

Okeanos' 3000 daughters were the Oceanids, while the Potamoi were his sons. They were river gods, sometimes depicted as humans, typically with water vessels, and sometimes as bulls with the heads of men or men with bull heads and serpentine tails. Each of the Potamoi was associated with a particular river, although some rivers, notably the Styx, were associated with goddesses instead. The most notable of the Potamoi was

LEUKOTHEA AND MELICARTES

Leukothea was a mortal who became a god through unfortunate circumstances. She was originally named Ino; along with her husband King Athamas she was charged with the protection and upbringing of the baby Dionysus, who was delivered to them by Hermes. Hera was jealous of her husband's illegitimate child and had already tried to have him killed by the Titans, who tore him apart. Brought back to life by Rhea, Dionysus was sent away for his own protection, but this brought disaster upon his foster parents.

Hera made Athamas mad, and in his rage he slew one of his sons, Learchus. Ino took the other, Melicartes, and jumped into the sea to escape. They were saved by the sea gods, who raised them to divinity. Ino became the sea goddess Leukothea and Melicartes became Palaemon. Both appear to have thought kindly of mariners; Leukothea assisted Odysseus when he was in danger and both are said to have rescued endangered sailors.

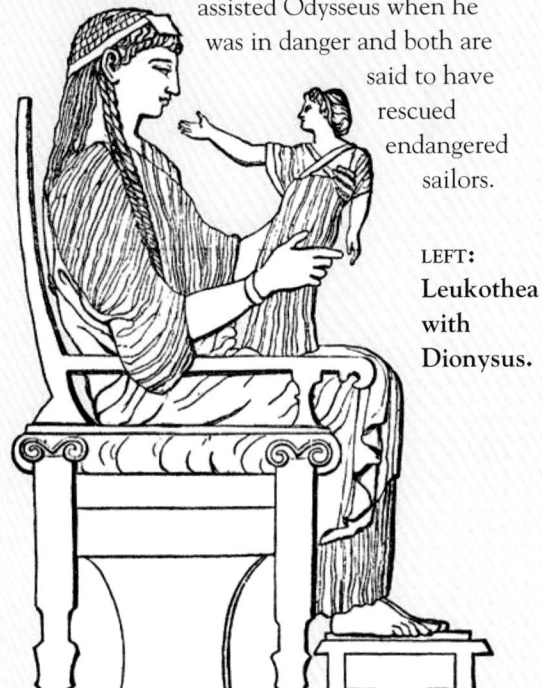

LEFT: Leukothea with Dionysus.

Acheron, god of the river that flowed through both Hades and the mortal world. Like some other mythical rivers, the Acheron was thought to connect to the surface world, in this case in northeast Greece.

Sky and Wind Gods

Helios, Eos and Selene were the children of Titans who continued in their roles as sun, dawn and moon after the ascension of the Olympians to power. They do not appear to have been greatly troubled by the events of the Titanomachy, and fitted into the new order as comfortably as they did the old. Helios was one of only two gods (Hecate, another former Titan, was the other) to see what had happened to Persephone when she was abducted by Hades. It is noted in this myth that Helios saw everything from his place in the sky, including the underhand dealings of Zeus in Olympus itself.

Some characters appear in multiple myths, where they are portrayed at times as a god and at others as a mortal. Several myths exist concerning Aeolus, keeper of the winds, which may refer to different beings of the same name or an evolution of the character from a mortal into a god as the stories changed over time. Homer describes Aeolus as a mortal who gave a bag containing the four winds to Odysseus. Later myths present Aeolus as a god, the son of Poseidon.

This later, godly, Aeolus had four children: the north, south, east and west winds. Their mother was Eos, goddess of the dawn, and collectively they were known as the Anemoi. Zephyrus, the west wind, was the gentlest of them – although he was still capable of killing Hyacinthus in a jealous rage – while Eurus, the east wind, was generally considered to be unlucky. Boreas the north wind brought cold winter weather, while Notus was a hot wind from the south that could ruin crops.

ABOVE: Helios was one of the Titans who were absorbed into the Olympian pantheon without conflict, probably because he fulfilled such an important function that he could not be replaced.

Chione was a daughter of Boreas, and was associated with snow. She had a child by Poseidon but was afraid of her father's reaction, so she threw the baby in the sea. Whether or not she hoped Poseidon would take care of it, he did. The child, named Eumolpus, was given to Poseidon's daughter Benthesikyme to raise, and later married one of her children. Eumolpus thus started out as the child of a sky god, was raised in Ethiopia by a sea god and eventually became a priest of Demeter.

Atlas, originally a Titan, is generally considered to be a sky god in Greek mythology. He was a leader in the war against the Olympians, and for this he was sentenced to hold the sky aloft for all eternity. Some sources state instead that he was appointed guardian of the Pillars of Heaven. Atlas is also credited with teaching mortals astronomy, enabling them to navigate at sea and to predict the changing seasons. In some myths, Atlas was turned into the mountains; in others, the Pillars of Hercules were built by the hero of that name, who had taken over Atlas' task for a time.

Iris, goddess of the rainbow, was a child of sea and sky. Her father was Thaumas, a sea god; her mother was Elektra, an Oceanid nymph associated with storm clouds illuminated by the sun. Iris became the handmaid of Hera, and

ABOVE: **Atlas is depicted holding up the world, but it was the sky that rested on his shoulders.**

THE PLANETS

The Astra Planeta, or planets, were children of the Titan Astreus and Eos, goddess of the dawn. Their other children were the Anemoi, or winds. Five planets were known to exist at the time, distinguished from stars by their patterns of movement. Venus was at times identified separately as Eosphorus, the morning star, and Hesperos, the evening star. The Hesperides, nymphs of the evening, were the descendants of Hesperos.

The planet Mercury was known as Stilbon and Mars as Pyroeis; Jupiter was named Phaethon, and may or may not have been the same being as Phaethon who borrowed Helios' sun-chariot and accidentally set fire to much of Libya. Phaenon was probably Saturn but the name has also been applied to Jupiter.

The nature of the planets was not known at the time, and their name essentially translates as 'wandering star'. The movements of the planets against the backdrop of the constellations posed many problems for early Greek scientists and philosophers, who had to construct a complex multi-layered sky dome to account for them.

acted as a messenger. She did not have stories of her own but appeared in the tales of other, more active, gods.

OPPOSITE: Iris is one of only two Greek gods who retained their names when adopted by the Romans. As the goddess of the rainbow she carried messages but apparently did not interfere in the affairs of mortals.

Nymphs and Satyrs

Nymphs were powerful spirits or minor deities, always female, who were associated with different aspects of the natural world. In general they were friendly and well disposed towards others; there are numerous tales of nymphs rescuing gods and heroes, or helping those who passed by. As attractive young females they were often the object of desire by gods and mortals alike. Several heroes were born as a result of relations between a major deity and a nymph, and some of the gods took nymphs as their wives.

LEFT: Nymphs are often depicted as desirable yet chaste, willing to go to almost any lengths to escape their godly suitors. Arethusa became a spring in Sicily in order to evade the river-god Alpheius.

Not all of these courtships succeeded. Arethusa was one of Artemis' band of friends, all of whom were determined to remain chaste. She came to the attention of the river god Alpheius while bathing in his waters, and he pursued her in human form when she refused his advances. Arethusa fled all the way to Sicily but could not escape Alpheius, so she asked Artemis for help. The goddess turned Arethusa into a spring, placing her beyond Alpheius' reach.

There were many kinds of nymph, of varying power and influence, and they are usually grouped according to their association with water, mountains and the like, which corresponds to their parentage. Thus, the descendants of Okeanos tended to be associated with water in various ways – streams, rivers and seas.

Oceanids

The Oceanids were the 3000 daughters of Okeanos, the Titan associated with the world-river and thus the source of all the world's waters. Some sources consider only the nymphs associated with the open seas to be Oceanids, while others use the term for all water nymphs including those associated with freshwater sources such as streams and springs. Water nymphs were closely associated with their body of water and depended upon it for survival. If their stream or spring dried up the nymph ceased to exist.

The most important and powerful Oceanids are also considered to be Titans, as they were among the children of the Titans born before the Olympian gods usurped their place in the universe. Metis, first wife of Zeus, was one of them, as was his third wife, Eurynome. Later generations are simply considered nymphs.

Naiades

Naiades were freshwater nymphs, who were also protectors of girls and young women. They were the daughters of the Potamoi, or river gods who were in turn descended from Okeanos and Tethys. The Naiades were further subdivided according to their association: Limnades ware associated with lakes and Potameides

with rivers. The Pegaiai were associated with springs, the Krenaiai with fountains and the Heleionomai with wetlands.

Nereids

The Nereids were the 50 daughters of Nereus and Doris. As sea nymphs they were generally well disposed towards mortals and would assist distressed sailors at times. Each personified an aspect of the sea or a skill needed by mariners and fishermen. The greatest of the Nereids were Amphitrite, wife of Poseidon, and Thetis, the mother of Achilles. Thetis appears to have been very loyal to Zeus, saving him from a rebellion by some of the other Olympians, and helped other gods when they needed it. In return, she was able to obtain assistance for her son during the Trojan Wars, although ultimately she was unable to save him.

Thetis and Peleus

Thetis was the subject of a prophecy that her son would be greater than his father. This would be a serious problem for Zeus if he

ABOVE: The parentage of nymphs generally dictated their associations. The Naiades were descended through the Potamoi, or river-gods, from Okeanos who was the source of all waters, fresh and salty.

or any major god fathered a child upon her. His answer was to insist that she marry a mortal. He chose Peleus, son of the king of Aegina. Peleus was not, by all accounts, a good man, although some of his troubles were not of his own making. With his brother Telamon he had slain their half-brother Phocus, which forced him to leave Aegina. Absolved of the crime, he married Antigone, who was the daughter of King Eurytion of Pthea in Thessaly.

Peleus was forced to flee again after accidentally killing his

RIGHT: Thetis, leader of the Nereids, fell victim to Zeus' paranoia. Fearing the potential of a child who was greater than his godly father, Zeus ensured that Thetis was married to the rather unpleasant mortal Peleus.

father-in-law during the Calydonian boar hunt. At Iolcus, King Acastus absolved him of this killing and he appears to have acted honourably when Acastus' wife Astydameia made advances. In revenge, Astydameia told Peleus' wife Antigone that her daughter was to be wed to Peleus and claimed to her husband that Peleus had been the one making advances.

Antigone killed herself out of grief and King Acastus arranged for Peleus to be left alone in the wilderness while

OPPOSITE: **Orpheus almost succeeded in rescuing his wife Eurydice from death, but the deals made by Hades were immutable. One backward glance was sufficient to allow Hades to reclaim Eurydice.**

they were out hunting. He was attacked by centaurs, but, for reasons best known to himself, Kheiron, leader of the centaurs, saved Peleus. Peleus took vengeance upon Acastus and Astydameia.

This was the man Zeus chose as a husband for Thetis, which seems a poor repayment for her loyalty and assistance when no-one else would help him. Worse, Zeus instructed Peleus to ambush and essentially rape Thetis. They were then married in a ceremony attended by all the gods, which in turn resulted in the Trojan Wars when Eris – who was not invited but forced her way in anyway – flung a golden apple into the wedding and invited the fairest goddess to claim it.

Thetis' marriage to Peleus did not last. He tried to interfere in her attempts to make her son, Achilles, immortal and invulnerable, which Thetis found intolerable. Achilles went on to be the foremost warrior of his age, fighting and ultimately dying in the war started at his parents' wedding. He did indeed surpass his father in prowess and greatness.

Dryads

Most nymphs seem to have been content to live a peaceful life in the countryside. Nymphs associated with trees were known as Dryads. Like water nymphs, they could not survive without their associated natural feature; if a tree died its dryad would also perish. Oreiades were associated with the mountains and the conifers that grew there, while the Napaea were to be found in valleys, glens and grottoes.

Dryads and similar nymphs were playful and generally harmless, and were often the wives or lovers of gods and heroes. The nymph Eurydice was the wife of Orpheus who became famous for his ability to charm even grim Hades with his music. When Eurydice died of a snakebite, Orpheus journeyed to the underworld to reclaim her. He was almost successful; his songs achieved what no prayers or sacrifice ever could, and Hades agreed to allow Eurydice to return to the upper world on condition that Orpheus walked in front of her and did not look back. He did so at the boundary of Hades' realm and Eurydice was lost to him.

Aurae

Nymphs associated with the breezes were termed Aurae. They are variously described as being the children of Okeanos or Boreas the north wind. Eos, goddess of the dawn, is sometimes described as being one of the Aurae. The sunset and evening were associated with the Hesperides, who were either the daughters of Atlas or of Nyx, primordial goddess of night. Among their tasks was caring for the tree of golden apples given to Hera on the day of her wedding to Zeus. They lived on the island of Erytheia in the western Mediterranean.

Satyrs

The male equivalent of the nymphs were satyrs, normally depicted as men with some features of animals such as tails and ears like those of an ass. Satyrs were particularly associated with Dionysus, Pan and Hermes. They seem to have been in a state of near-constant sexual arousal and are often depicted that way. Some satyrs (Panes) had the legs and sometimes the head of a goat and were particularly sexually active.

Many notable satyrs appear within the Greek myths. These include Silenus, mentor to Dionysus and a patron of drunks, who appears in the story of King Midas. The Lenae were part of the entourage of Dionysus, and were in charge of wine-making, while Ampelos was transformed by Dionysus into the very first grapevine after being killed by a bull.

Misfit Gods

Some gods did not fit neatly into the Greek pantheon. Hecate was one of them, being the child of the Titans Perses and Asteria. Some tales of the Titanomachy state that all of the Titans, with the exception of certain named individuals, fought against the Olympians and were imprisoned in Tartarus for it. Yet a number of deities appear unaffected by the conflict and appear to have joined the Olympians without incident.

It seems that Hecate was an older deity co-opted by the Ancient Greeks, becoming dark and mysterious as a result of new myths and legends. Hecate was associated with the night and with magic, particularly witchcraft. Although a rather grim

ECHO AND NARCISSUS

Echo was a nymph who was part of the retinue of Artemis. She liked to talk and always got the last word. Echo was given the task of stalling Hera, who was looking for Zeus and correctly suspected he could be found among the wood nymphs. Echo was successful, but Hera punished her with a curse. Henceforth Echo could only reply and would never be able to speak first.

Echo met her end when she fell in love with Narcissus, a handsome young man who was not interested in her or any of the other nymphs. Echo wanted to approach him but could not speak first, and when Narcissus finally did speak to her she could only reply with an echo of his words. Rejected by her love, Echo hid away in a cave until she died, leaving behind only her ability to get the last word by echoing what others had spoken. Echo in turn caused distress to King Midas. Apollo and Pan held a musical contest, and most of the judges sided with Apollo. King Midas did not, and as punishment Apollo gave him a set of ears like those of an ass. This was, Apollo said, to allow him to hear music properly in future.

Midas was embarrassed of his ears and concealed them with a variety of hats. Only his barber ever saw his ears. The barber kept the secret for many years, but eventually the compulsion to tell someone became overwhelming. His solution was to dig a hole and speak his secret into the ground, but unfortunately he was heard by Echo and his words were repeated all across the kingdom.

As to Narcissus, he continued to spurn the advances of the nymphs. One in particular prayed for vengeance, asking that Narcissus might know what it was to love someone without being loved in return. Narcissus saw his own reflection in a pool of water and became enamoured of it, thinking it a water spirit. Narcissus could not touch his reflection no matter how hard he tried. He remained by the pool, pining away out of love for himself, until he died. The nymphs came to take his body for a funeral but found only the flowers now known as Narcissus. In an alternative version of the tale, the spurned lover was a man named Arminias, who committed suicide while asking the gods for vengeance.

BELOW: Narcissus' fascination with his own reflection was inflicted upon him rather than it being his own choice.

RIGHT: Asclepius and his wife (or daughter) Hygeia were great benefactors of humanity, and indeed they may have been too successful for their own good. Zeus slew Asclepius in order to keep mortals in their place.

and frightening goddess, she was a good friend to Demeter, lighting her way in the night with torches as the two searched for Persephone. She also fought well for Olympus during the Gigantomachy.

Nemesis and Tyche were also important gods who did not fit neatly into the pantheon. Tyche is normally considered to be a child of Okeanos and Tethys. Nemesis, born of Okeanos or Nyx, was in some ways her opposite, and they were often depicted together.

Tyche was associated with good and bad fortune, although some of her aspects were connected only with good luck and unexpected bounty. She was given the credit for unexpectedly good fortune, and was the subject of many requests that a mortal's luck might turn around or that some stroke of fortune might get that person out of a bad situation.

Nemesis represented the feeling of resentment at someone else's undeservedly good fortune or those who apparently escaped retribution for their crimes. One of her functions was to ensure that Tyche did not bestow an excess of good luck upon mortals, and to rebalance the scales with sorrow or loss if an individual was having it too good. She also brought retribution in a more direct manner against those who committed crimes and remained unrepentant.

Asclepius was the son of Apollo, although his mother's identity varies from one myth to another. In some stories, his mother was Coronis, who was either killed for infidelity by Apollo or abandoned her child to be raised by animals. Apollo looked after the baby and taught him about medicine, and later the centaur Kheiron was his tutor.

Asclepius is said to have married Hygeia, a goddess associated with health – though in some myths she is his daughter. His other children founded a dynasty of great healers who included the mortal 'father of medicine', Hippocrates. Asclepius himself was slain by Zeus, who was apparently worried that sufficiently good medical care might enable mortals to erode the barriers between their existence and godhood. Zeus killed Asclepius with a thunderbolt and punished Apollo for protesting, but did not prevent mortals from creating several holy places connected with healing in his honour.

BELOW: **Ariadne was the daughter of king Minos of Crete, and assisted Theseus in finding his way through the labyrinth to slay the Minotaur. In some versions of her story she was abandoned on Naxos by Theseus.**

Minor Gods and Retinues

Many of the Greek gods and spirits are important only by association with a more powerful deity. Some have a story that can be pieced together, but for the most part they feature only in the myths of others. This may be their partner-gods or heroes who encounter the deity in their travels. These gods and spirits occupy a niche in Greek mythology that might be equivalent to the supporting cast or even the extras in a movie or television show.

The retinue of Dionysus

Dionysus was an important god with many aspects, and had his own significant myths. His wife Ariadne, on the other hand, appears only by association with others. Sources differ on how Ariadne came to be Dionysus' partner. In one version she was slain during a battle and rescued from Hades by Dionysus; in another she helped the hero Theseus to defeat the Minotaur in her father's domain on Crete. She was rather badly treated by Theseus, who abandoned her on the island of Naxos. Dionysus found her there and made her his wife. Again there are conflicting versions of the tale; in some Dionysus brought her to Olympus; in others she was slain by Artemis.

Dionysus was attended by a retinue of women named Maenads, who may have been spirits or women possessed by them. They could bring forth milk or wine from the ground, but were also capable of great fury. Maenads could not be harmed by the weapons of mortals, and were at times sent against the enemies of Dionysus. Satyrs also formed part of the retinue of Dionysus. Among them was Silenus, an extremely old satyr who was a mentor and tutor to the god.

The retinue of Zeus

As king of the gods, Zeus could count most of the other deities of Olympus as his retinue, but he did have several close companions who carried out specific tasks for him. His four most trusted were all children of Styx, who had been an early ally in the Titanomachy; his children were bound to Zeus by oaths made on the river Styx.

Kratos and Bia were warriors who guarded Zeus' throne and captured Prometheus after he stole fire from Olympus. Kratos represented warlike strength and Bia force; it seems they had no other function than to guard Zeus and enforce his will. Zelus, representing zeal and dedication, was similarly committed. Their sister Nike played a greater role in cosmic affairs, as Zeus' charioteer and the arbiter of victory. Nike had the ability to award victory or avert defeat and was worshipped by warriors.

Hebe, daughter of Zeus and Hera, was the goddess of youth and served in Olympus as a cup-bearer. This was a sensitive post, as it gave her access to the ambrosia and nectar served to the gods. Zeus himself held the same position as cup-bearer to Chronos, which allowed him to hatch his plot to overthrow the Titans.

Hebe was able to restore youth and vigour, and once did so for Iolaus, charioteer to Heracles, before a fight with Eurystheus. She eventually married Heracles and bore him two children, but lost her post as cup-bearer as the result of an unfortunate incident in which her dress came open while she was serving nectar to the gods.

It is not clear why this upset the gods sufficiently to dismiss Hebe, but her duties were taken over by Ganymede. He was originally a mortal, a prince of Troy who was taken to Olympus by Zeus. There seems to have been no reason for this, other perhaps than the fact that Ganymede was the most beautiful of all mortals. It would not be beyond the selfishness of the gods, especially Zeus, to pluck a mortal from earth simply to serve as eye candy in Olympus.

ABOVE: Hebe held an influential post in Olympus until dismissed by Zeus over an incident that seems quite trivial. It is hard to imagine that Zeus found the sight of Hebe's breasts upsetting, especially given his lustful nature.

BELOW: Ganymede was the most beautiful of all mortals, so Zeus sent an eagle to carry him away to Olympus where he would serve as cup-bearer. Mortals seem to have been little more than playthings to the Olympians.

The Oneiroi

Ganymede became a minor god associated with homosexual love, part of a group that included Eros and Hymenaios, god of weddings. Several such groupings existed, often but not always with the same parents. The Oneiroi, daemones associated with dreams, were one such group. Variously described as the children of Nyx and Erebus (or just Nyx alone) or Hypnos, god of sleep, the Oneiroi are described as dark-winged spirits who lived in a cave.

Sources vary on how many Oneiroi there were, and only a handful are named. In some versions, the Oneiroi flew through gates of horn or ivory when they left their cave; which gate a spirit used determined whether the dreams it brought would be useful, false or nonsensical. At times the gods used the Oneiroi to carry messages to mortals.

The leader of the Oneiroi is sometimes named as Morpheus, and was able to take on human form in dreams. Phobetor brought frightening dreams, while Phantasos was associated with inanimate objects and strange, confusing dreams that might mean nothing at all.

If Hypnos, god of sleep, was also a child of Nyx then he was brother to the Oneiroi but presumably more powerful since his area of interest was much wider than a single aspect of dreams. Thanatos, god of peaceful death, was the twin brother of Hypnos and had sisters of his own. These there the Keres, bloodthirsty killers by disease and violence. They are sometimes associated with the Nosoi, spirits who brought plagues and disease, but the connection is nebulous.

The Keres

The Keres could be over-zealous and – even though they were supposedly servants of the three Moirae – would sometimes ignore fate in their lust to slay someone. The best protection against these

ABOVE: Morpheus is the most widely known of the Oneiroi, and may be the only one capable of taking on human form. He is generally assumed to be the spirit who delivered Zeus' message to king Agamemnon in the *Iliad*.

unruly spirits was to have the patronage of a god, who would keep them away from a hero to prevent an untimely death. Those without such a patron would have to take their chances.

The Keres were children of Nyx and were commonly grouped together with other minor deities personifying the darker and more unpleasant aspects of life: Geras was associated with old age and Oizys with suffering. Moros was doom and Momos blame. Apate personified deceit and was the sister of Eris, who loved to cause dissent and strife. Her crowning achievement – if it could be called that – was the Trojan Wars, which provided many opportunities for the Keres to indulge their thirst for blood.

The Charites

Other groupings included the Charites, generally considered to be daughters of Zeus and his third wife Eurynome. Sources vary as to the number of the Charites, though some say there were three. Hesiod names three Charites: Aglea (glory, or splendour), Thalia (banquet) and Euphroyne (mirth).

Other writers add many more Charites, resulting in Hesiod's three being known as the Elder Charites and the additional spirits as the Younger Charites. They were not the subject of their own stories but formed part of the retinue of various gods including Apollo, Aphrodite and Hera.

Giants and Gods

Giants appear in many of the Greek myths, presumably because gods require suitable foes to make their deeds seem impressive. As well as providing thunderbolt-fodder for the Gigantomachy, the race of giants included a number of notable individuals.

Tityos

The giant Tityos was born under unusual circumstances. He was the child of Zeus and a mortal princess named Elara. More concerned with concealing his infidelity from Hera than the well-being of his lover, Zeus buried her in the ground.

The Muses

The Muses were similar to the Charites in many ways. They are normally considered to be the daughters of Zeus and Mnemosyne, goddess of memory. Originally the Muses seem to have been a personification of memory or knowledge, but over time each came to be associated with a different facet of the arts. Kleio was associated with history, perhaps retaining her original area of expertise, while Ourania was the Muse of astronomy and Kalliope of epic poetry. Euterpe was associated with lyrical poetry while Erato was concerned with erotic poems. Thaleia was the Muse of comedy and Melpomene of tragedy; Polymenia was concerned with religious music and Terpsichore with song and dance.

BELOW: **The Muses personified facets of the arts, and it was not safe to compare a mortal's talent to theirs.**

This caused the baby, Tityos, to grow to enormous size and then be birthed inside Gaea. Elara presumably perished at some point in this process, since Gaea then carried the baby for a time.

Tityos was born a giant. There are no records of the deeds of his life until, apparently at the behest of Hera, he tried to rape Leto in Panopeus. Hera may have been trying to take revenge for Leto's relationship with Zeus, which produced Apollo and Artemis, but Tityos was thwarted by the twin gods. Tityos was chained to a rock in Tartarus so that vultures could eat his liver every day. Like Prometheus, he regrew his organ overnight, enabling the punishment to go on forever.

It is notable that Tityos was savagely punished for attempted rape, whereas the Olympian gods carried out numerous such crimes and apparently thought nothing of it. It seems that – according to Zeus at least – the crime was not Tityos' act or intentions, but the fact that they were directed at someone who had the gods' favour.

BELOW: Not all giants were enemies of the Olympians. Argus Panoptes served Hera faithfully, watching over Io (in heifer form) with his hundred eyes. He was murdered in his sleep by Hermes in order to conceal Zeus' latest infidelity.

RIGHT: Tityos was savagely punished for the most serious crime possible in the Olympian cosmos – being an enemy of the gods. His fate was similar to that of Prometheus, perhaps due to a writer's confusion between the two tales.

The Aloadai

Two giants named Otus and Ephilates performed heroic deeds in their youth, but ultimately fell foul of the gods. They are commonly referred to as Aloadai, since their mother's husband (and ostensible father) was named Aloeus, but they were fathered by Poseidon. This resulted in superhuman size and prowess, enabling the giants to rescue their mother from pirates and perform other worthy deeds.

According to some sources, the Aloadai then decided to storm Olympus. This was to be accomplished by piling up mountains on top of one another. Their efforts were thwarted by Apollo, who shot and killed the Aloadai, after which Zeus demolished the mountain-ramp with his thunderbolts.

It may have been that the purpose of Otus and Ephilates was to take control of Olympus and oust Zeus, but some sources say they wished to take Artemis and Hera as their wives. This concept appears in another version of the tale, in which the giants captured Ares and imprisoned him in a bronze urn. None of the gods noticed Ares was missing at first, and it was many months before a search began. Eventually Hermes found him and – in some versions – secured his release.

An alternative version of the tale has Artemis offering herself in return for Ares' release, which set the giants to arguing. In the middle of the row, Artemis turned herself into a stag, and both giants threw their spears to prevent her from escaping. Naturally, they hit one another and were both slain.

The Aloadai met the same fate as many others who challenged the gods – they were condemned to be tormented in Tartarus. In their case, they were tied to pillars using snakes, and an owl was set to shriek at them endlessly.

It is clear that the gods' moral code was not so much guided by a sense of right and wrong, but of vengeance for offences against them. In the case of the Aloadai, whether they sought to overthrow Zeus or take goddesses as their wives, the crime was the same – the Aloadai challenged the supremacy of Zeus and his Olympians, and that could not be tolerated.

Argus Panoptes

Among the giants was Argus Panoptes, who had 100 eyes. He was appointed by Hera to watch over a white heifer that she correctly suspected was more than it seemed.

The heifer was in fact the nymph Io, transformed by Zeus to conceal his latest infidelity. Seeking to penetrate her husband's deception, Hera requested the fine animal as a gift, and Zeus could hardly refuse. This left Io trapped in heifer form and the possibility that Hera would uncover the deception or perhaps just keep Io like that forever, pretending she thought the animal was simply a fine possession.

Zeus sent Hermes to deal with the problem, which meant getting the all-seeing Argus Panoptes out of the way. His solution was to lull the giant to sleep with music then decapitate him, which was effective if not especially creative. Io was thus freed and Argus Panoptes was later rewarded by Hera, who placed his eyes on the tail of the peacock, a bird sacred to her. A missing heifer and a decapitated guardian might have aroused some suspicion, but nothing further seems to have come of it.

THE WORLD OF GODS AND MORTALS

The idea that mortals and gods shared the world and could interact was central to Greek mythology. Many of these interactions were one-sided, although often the intrigues of one god could get a mortal out of the terrible situation he or she had been put in by another.

Some humans were notable enough to attract the attention of the gods, and some were even able to make demands of them.

The most mundane part of the world was that close to home. Even then, the works of the gods could be seen in the marketplace and the fields outside a town. A sudden and unexplained death might be attributed to the arrows of Artemis; the blossoming of plants or the coming of cold winter weather were wrought by the actions of the gods.

There were also mythical or supernatural places within the world experienced by the average Ancient Greek citizen. Oracles, streams associated with various myths and sites where

OPPOSITE: The idea that gods and mythical creatures – Athena and the centaur Kheiron in this case – could be encountered by a lost traveller or unfortunate mariner was central to Ancient Greek mythology.

the gods fought giants in the relatively recent past lay by the roadside or on islands passed by merchant ships going about their mundane business. These were places to be respected at least, and feared by those who were wise. Few interactions with the gods ended well for mortals.

Further afield were real places known of only by their legendary reputation. Beyond those were the lands of myth, where strange people and creatures might be encountered by those brave enough to venture there. This was the world inhabited by the Ancient Greeks; one where mysterious and supernatural creatures existed just over the horizon and barely outside living memory.

Mapping the Known World

By around 300BC, the Ancient Greeks had compiled a reasonably accurate map of the lands around the Mediterranean. Increasing distance – or, more accurately, greater travel time – from Greece corresponded to a reduction in accuracy, but a Greek map of 300BC showed Europe, Persia and even India in general terms. The Ancient Greeks were aware of some regions only at second or third hand, but they had a reasonable idea of their place in the world.

To the northeast of Greece lay the land of the Thracians, which was fairly well known to the Ancient Greeks; beyond that was the home of the Scythians. North and northwest were

RIGHT: Greek mariners regularly plied the coastal trade routes around the Mediterranean and the Black Sea. Routes between major cities were well known, but there were plenty of mysterious islands and uncharted waters, and the open sea held many mysteries.

lands inhabited by people known to the Greeks as 'Keltoi', which essentially meant 'barbarians'. They also inhabited much of Europe.

Across the Aegean Sea to the east lay Asia Minor, Persia, Arabia and eventually India; Egypt lay to the south. The African lands west of Egypt were known as Libya, and to the south of that was Ethiopia. Greek travellers had visited some of these places and met people there who had been further afield. Maps of the era are often rather vague about where any particular region lay, but this is hardly surprising. They had been compiled at least in part from hearsay, and pieced together from a knowledge of key points such as islands, trade routes and cities.

The cultural interchange between Greece and Egypt was constant, resulting in similarities between some gods and religious practices. After the creation of Alexander the Great's empire, Egypt was essentially a Greek state and traditional Egyptian influences waned in importance. Similarly, the 'Keltoi', known in modern times as Celts, of Europe were constant trade partners. The Celts had no written language of their own, other than inscriptions on stones, but in some cases used Greek when written communications or records were required.

Similarly, trade with Persia and with the lands of the Scythians was a constant factor. As a result, some gods have equivalents from other cultures, and in many cases there are similar myths concerning the deities of what are ostensibly

ABOVE: The centaurs were native to Thessaly, though there were stories of other groups elsewhere, and similar half-man, half-beast creatures featured in many tales of more distant lands.

entirely different religions. It was of course not just myths that were exchanged; news and rumours of far-off places filtered into the cities of Ancient Greece aboard merchant ships or along overland trade routes. Considerable knowledge of the outside world was available to the citizens of Greece, though naturally some of it was distorted.

Mapping the Mythical World

Beyond the well-travelled regions – which became increasingly less well known with distance from Greece – were places of myth and rumour. The Ancient Greeks believed there was a land named Hyperborea somewhere in the north of Europe, and beyond that there were islands in the encircling sea including the mythical Thule. This attempt at a mundane-world map did not entirely clash with the mythic version.

The vast Atlantic Ocean had a coastline curving away to the north and south outside the Pillars of Hercules, and was presumed to encircle the world just as the world-river Okeanos did in legend. Distant lands were known of only through rumour and travellers' tales, and there were enough vague areas on the map that any of the legendary lands could be fitted in without difficulty. The location of some of these lands were known for certain, though the details of what lay there were distorted by legend.

Even within the known lands there was room for wonder and strangeness. The half-man, half-horse centaurs lived in Thessaly, the region of eastern Greece where Mount Olympus lay. They were the children of a nymph named Nephele and King Ixion, a bad character whose sister Coronis was a lover of Apollo and mother to Asclepius, god of medicine.

The centaurs inherited much of their father's nature. They were bestial and primitive, much given to rage and violence. Despite this, the original centaur, Kheiron, tried to watch over them. He was the child of the Titan Chronos, and father to a more refined group of centaurs. He was not very successful in safeguarding his brethren, however; most of them died in a pointless fight at a wedding. Other groups of centaurs lived in the Peloponnese, and there was a bull-horned tribe on Cyprus. The origin of these tribes is unclear.

The Amazons

The Amazons, an all-female warrior tribe, were said to live somewhere north of the Black Sea. Some sources place their homeland in the Caucasus Mountains, close to the lands of the all-male Gargarean tribe. In some versions of the story, the two tribes met annually to procreate and seem to have had good relations. In other tales, the tribes were enemies who abducted victims and used them, either killing the captives or enslaving them.

The Amazons are said to have removed the right breast of their children, so that it would not interfere with the use of their bows. They are generally depicted dressed in Greek style, sometimes with Persian influences, and armed with axes, bows and spears. They are credited with founding some of the Greek cities, but appear as opponents of Heracles, Theseus and Bellerophon.

BELOW: **The Amazons feature in several myths, often as opponents of Greek heroes, but there do not seem to be any tales from their perspective.**

Creatures and People of the Islands

The many islands of the Aegean, Ionian and Mediterranean were home to strange creatures, some of which were encountered by lost mariners or unwise explorers. A tribe of six-armed giants was said to live on the southern coast of the Propontis, now known as the Sea of Marmara, which lies between the Black Sea and the Aegean. They were encountered by Jason and his Argonauts, and may have attacked other travellers in the region.

BELOW: **All Cyclopes are assumed to have one eye, though only Polyphemus is described this way. They were violent and brutish people who supplemented their diet with human flesh when it was available.**

The island of Hyperea (generally assumed to be Sicily) was home to the Cyclopes. There were only three original Cyclopes, who were sons of the Titan Chronos. One of them, Polyphemus, went to live on Hyperea and was joined by other, lesser, Cyclopes created when Uranus' blood fell upon the land. Although less powerful than Polyphemus they were still huge and powerful creatures. The Cyclopes lived a primitive existence as herdsmen, living in caves in the mountains and gathering what they needed from the land rather than farming it.

The Phaiakians, a peaceable people who were great mariners, described themselves as being 'close of kin' with the Cyclopes. This is generally supposed to mean that the Phaiakians were also created when Uranus was castrated, rather than sharing any physical similarity. The Phaiakians once also inhabited Hyperea but wearied of being raided by the more powerful Cyclopes. They relocated their home to an island named Skheria, which, from references made in Homer's *Odyssey*, seems to have been close to mainland Greece.

Creatures of the Seas

The seas were, of course, inhabited by a vast array of completely mundane creatures, but in addition there existed a number of magical species and powerful spirits. Among them were the Hippokampoi, fish-tailed horses who pulled Poseidon's chariot and acted as mounts for water spirits and gods. Other fish-tailed versions of land creatures were said to exist, including lions and goats. Immature Hippokampoi (in other words, what are today called seahorses) could be encountered in familiar waters, but many of the more exotic species were native to distant areas such as the Erythreaen Sea – today called the Indian Ocean.

The term 'Ketea' was used in general to describe large sea creatures such as whales, but also more specifically to refer to fearsome monsters sent by Poseidon to terrorize coastal cities. One was slain by Perseus, another by Heracles, and presumably Greek mariners feared they might encounter one any time they ventured on to the open sea without proper sacrifices to Poseidon.

Other sea-monsters were individuals. Kharybdis may have been a daughter of Pontus and Gaea, or perhaps a mortal woman who was turned into a sea monster. Either way, she was flung into the sea and possibly chained in place by Zeus, and created a savage whirlpool in the Strait of Messina between Italy and Sicily. Opposite Kharybdis in the strait lived Scylla, who had twelve feet

ABOVE: Proof that the Hippokampoi – fish-tailed horses who pulled Poseidon's chariot – existed was readily available. What are today called seahorses could be found in the waters around Greece, and were assumed to be immature Hippokampoi.

OPPOSITE: **Heracles slew many of the children of Typhon and Echidna, including the brother of Kerberos, the two-headed Orthus. Kerberos himself was spared, presumably due to his service to Hades and the Olympian gods.**

and six heads on long necks. Ships that passed close to her rocks in order to avoid Kharybdis' whirlpool were attacked by Scylla, who seized six men at a time from the deck and ate them.

Monsters and Creatures of the Underworld

Most of the monsters of Ancient Greek mythology were descended from Typhon, a hundred-headed dragon-giant who all but defeated Zeus in their first battle. Typhon's parents were Gaea and Tartarus; he was a terrifying mix of all the horrors the natural world and the underworld held.

Although Typhon tore out Zeus' tendons, Hermes – or possibly Aigipan, one of the Panes – was able to get them back for him, and the monster was eventually defeated by Zeus' thunderbolts. Typhon was imprisoned under Mount Etna in Sicily, but his wife Echidna and their children were allowed to survive. Echidna was half-woman, half-snake and probably the most deadly monster in all the cosmos. Like Typhon, she was the child of Gaea and Tartarus, and together they were the parents or ancestors of many terrifying creatures.

Kerberos and Orthrus

Most famous of the creatures of the Greek underworld was Kerberos, the three-headed hound of Hades. Often depicted as a dog, Kerberos may have been some other type of creature serving a similar function. He is sometimes described as having 50 heads rather than three; this may be a reference to his mane of serpents. Some sources also give him a serpentine tail and the claws of a lion. Kerberos was not inimical to gods or mortals, although he would prevent anyone leaving the realm of Hades by whatever means proved necessary.

Kerberos had an older brother, Orthrus, who was a two-headed dog. Orthrus lived on the island of Erythea with the giant Geryon, who had three heads and either one or three bodies. The giant and the hound were among the guardians of the garden of the Hesperides, where Hera's golden apples grew. The dragon Ladon was also placed there to protect the garden; some sources name Ladon as a descendant of Typhon and Echidna, while others postulate Keto and Phorcys as parents, or Gaea herself.

THE CHIMERA

The Chimera, a three-headed monster that terrorized Lycia in Asia Minor, was another child of Typhon and Echidna. It had the body of a lion, with a lion's head. A second head, that of a goat, grew from the Chimera's back. It also had a serpent for a tail and could breathe fire. The Chimera was eventually slain by Bellerophon.

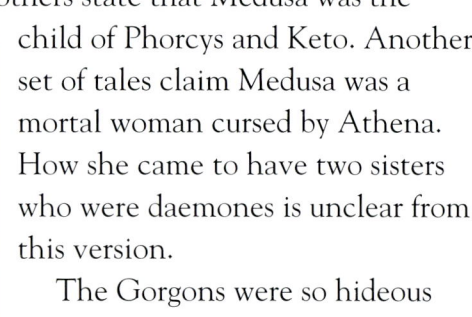

RIGHT: **The three-headed monster, Chimera.**

The Gorgons and Medusa

The familial relationships of some monsters could be complex. The Gorgons, or Gorgones, were three sisters named Euryale, Medusa and Stheno. According to some sources, the three Gorgons were part of a monstrous extended family descended from Typhon and Echidna; others state that Medusa was the child of Phorcys and Keto. Another set of tales claim Medusa was a mortal woman cursed by Athena. How she came to have two sisters who were daemones is unclear from this version.

The Gorgons were so hideous that any man looking upon their faces would be turned to stone. They are often depicted as winged women with hair of serpents and bestial features such as tusks, although sometimes Medusa is a beautiful woman with snakes for hair. Medusa was slain by Perseus and her head mounted on Athena's shield, but not before blood dripping from it turned into a vast number of snakes.

BELOW: **Tales of Medusa cannot agree on her appearance, but the central facets of snakes for hair and the ability to turn people to stone remain the same.**

Not all of Medusa's family were monsters. Upon her death, the winged horse Pegasus sprang from her neck. This noble creature served as a steed for Bellerophon when he battled the Chimera, and tried to take him to Olympus. Although Bellerophon fell back to earth, Pegasus made the flight and entered the service of Zeus as the bearer of his thunderbolts.

Medusa's other child was the warrior Chrysaor. He played little part in any myth, but is credited with being the father of the three-headed giant Geryon. Geryon's mother was an Oceanid named Callirrhoe. Some sources claim that Echidna – possibly Chrysaor's grandmother – was another of their children.

Bird monsters

Harpyai, usually depicted as part-woman, part-bird, may or may not have been intrinsically malevolent, but were sent by Zeus to pester and harass mortals. Among them was King Phineas of Thrace, who revealed the secrets of the gods and was punished with a plague of harpies who stole his food. Harpies also served Zeus by bringing him people and objects he desired, often without the lost person's friends and relatives having any idea what had happened to them.

The Sirens were also bird-women. Originally the handmaidens of Persephone, they were given the bodies of birds by Demeter. This enabled them to search for Persephone when she was abducted by Hades. Unsuccessful in their search, the Sirens made a home on the island of Anthemoessa, from where their song lured sailors to their death.

The Stymphalian Birds were unusual in that they were deliberately created by the gods. Ares, god of war, gave them poisonous dung, bronze beaks and feathers they could shoot at their enemies. The birds liked to devour humans, and laid waste to the area around Lake Stymphalia in Arcadia. After Heracles killed most of them they relocated to an island in the Black Sea, where they later encountered the Argonauts.

ABOVE: The Harpyai, or Harpies, were malevolent creatures used by Zeus to torment and occasionally capture mortals. They were defeated by the hero Jason during his quest for the Golden Fleece.

The Hydra

The serpentine, nine-headed Hydra – another child of Typhon and Echidna – lived in a marshy region in Lerna, part of the Peloponnese. Its home was Lake Lerna, which was one of the entrances to the underworld. Dionysus entered by this route when he went in search of his mother Semele, and mortals were said to be dragged under and lost if they ventured into its waters. The Hydra itself acted as guardian to the underworld and was thought to be unkillable as two heads grew from the stump every time one was severed. The Hydra was eventually slain by Heracles, who cauterized the stumps with fire and prevented more heads from springing forth.

After slaying the Hydra, Heracles used its blood as a poison on his arrows; this was in general extremely effective. However, his arrows could not harm the Nemean Lion. Generally considered to be another of Typhon's offspring, the lion is sometimes cited as being the child of Zeus and Selene. Its hide was impenetrable to weapons but it still needed to breathe. Heracles strangled the creature and – acting upon advice from Athena – skinned it using one of its own claws.

RIGHT: Advised by Iolaus to cauterize the stumps of the Hydra's severed necks, Heracles was able to prevent the monster from growing more heads, ultimately defeating it. The Hydra's blood was a potent weapon for Heracles thereafter.

The Minotaur and the Cretan Bull

The Minotaur was apparently not of divine origin, but was instead the child of Queen Pasiphae of Crete and a bull that came out of the sea. Usually depicted as a bull-headed man, the Minotaur is sometimes described as a bull with a man's head. It was imprisoned in a labyrinth designed by the great artificer Daedalus for King Minos, and fed on a diet of human sacrifices until slain by Theseus.

The Cretan Bull that fathered the Minotaur had a long and eventful career. Its origins are unknown, other than the fact that it emerged from the sea on Crete. This was taken as a sign that Minos, at that time a candidate for the throne of Crete, was favoured by Poseidon. Once he had been crowned, Minos would have sacrificed the bull, but decided it was too magnificent to waste. A lesser animal was sacrificed, which proved to be a dangerous course of action.

Poseidon was angered, and cursed Minos' wife Pasiphae to fall in love with the bull. Once it had fathered a child – the Minotaur – upon her, Poseidon sent it on a rampage around Crete that ended only when Heracles captured it as one of his labours. The bull was to have been sacrificed to Hera, but whether it escaped or she refused a sacrifice that was the work of Heracles, whom Hera still hated, the bull escaped and eventually made its way to Marathon.

The bull caused such destruction around Marathon that King Aegeus of Athens sought someone to deal with it. He chose Androgeus, son of King Minos of Crete. Androgeus was no Heracles, however, and was slain by the bull. This resulted in war between Athens and Crete, after which Athens had to pay an annual tribute of seven young men and seven young women to be sacrificed to the Minotaur. This continued until the hero Theseus slew the bull and later the Minotaur.

ABOVE: The true name of the Minotaur (which translates as 'bull of Minos') slain by Theseus was Asterion. The labyrinth in which he was housed was designed by the inventor Daedalus.

THE SPHINX

Like the Cretan Bull, another creature that fed upon the youth of a city was the Sphinx, with the body of a lion, head of a woman and wings of an eagle. Some accounts also give the Sphinx a serpent tail. The Sphynx was the daughter of Orthrus, two-headed brother of Kerberos, and Echidna or Chimera. It terrorized the city of Thebes, eating anyone who could not solve its riddle, until Oedipus did so. The Sphinx was so disappointed at being outwitted that it threw itself off a mountain. Other accounts have the Sphinx devour itself.

ABOVE: Rejected by his parents and left to die, Oedipus was rescued and had many adventures including his defeat of the Sphinx.

The horses of King Diomedes

Some monsters were created by the actions of mortals. For reasons that remain unclear, King Diomedes of Thrace fed four of his horses on human flesh. This turned them into crazed monsters that, in some versions of the myth, could also breathe fire. Heracles was sent to retrieve them as one of his labours, and managed to pacify them by feeding the horses enough human flesh – including that of their master Diomedes – that they were satisfied. Heracles offered the horses to Zeus as a sacrifice, but Zeus was not pleased and sent wild animals to kill them.

Artemis' boar

Monsters were used by the gods to punish mortals, often in an indiscriminate manner. When King Oeneus of Calydon forgot to include Artemis among the gods to receive the sacrifices that year, she sent a great boar to terrorize the countryside. The people of Calydon retreated within their walls, an action that saved their lives, but they could not work their fields and eventually starved to death.

The boar was a child of the Crommyonian Sow, a child of Typhon and Echidna that had devastated the land around Crommyon near Corinth until slain by Theseus. The gods were quite willing to send such creatures into the lands of mortals to take vengeance for one person's actions against anyone the beast encountered. The gods used their power this way because they could; there was no moral lesson in these stories, other than to

BELOW: Atalanta was one of the few powerful female figures – among mortals at least – in the Greek myths. Her slaying of the mighty Calydonian Boar was a mighty deed, but the jealous male warriors on the expedition refused to give her the beast's hide as a trophy.

avoid the wrath of the gods by regularly bribing them. Indeed, the relationship between mortals and gods at times resembles a protection racket more than the veneration of benevolent deities by their worshippers.

King Oeneus asked for help from anyone who would help him hunt the monstrous boar. Among those who came was Peleus, who would one day marry the nymph Thetis, and his father-in-law Eurytion. Their contribution was not auspicious: Peleus accidentally killed Eurytion with a spear. However, the sole woman on the expedition, Atalanta, dealt the boar a mortal wound with her bow. Atalanta was quite the warrior, and in the past had defended herself against centaurs, wrestled King Peleus into submission and sailed with the Argonauts.

When the boar was dead, Atalanta quite reasonably claimed its pelt as a trophy. She was supported by King Oeneus' son Meleager, who was in love with her. The king's brothers objected, and Meleager killed them in a rage. This brought about his own demise at the hands of his mother.

When Meleager was a week old, the Fates had appeared to his mother and prophesied that his life would end when a particular

BELOW: Meleager was invulnerable until a particular branch was burned away, which had enabled him to pursue a successful career as an adventurer and hero. His killing of several of the Calydonian boar hunters caused his mother to burn the branch.

stick in the fire had burned away. She immediately pulled the stick from the fire and doused it, hiding it away for safekeeping. Meleager went on to have a glittering career as a warrior, travelling with Jason and the Argonauts and having many adventures. However, when his mother learned of his deeds at the boar hunt she burned the branch and ended Meleager's life. There is an alternative version of this story in which the killing and the burning of the branch occurred as part of an old blood feud reignited by the dispute over the monstrous boar's hide.

BELOW: Heracles risked the notoriously bloody vengeance of Artemis when he hunted the Ceryneian Hind, but was able to negotiate a solution that allowed him to complete the labour without killing the beast.

Other monsters

The world of Ancient Greece had many other monsters, it seems, including a giant crab or perhaps even a species of them. One such creature, named Karkinos, tried to help the Hydra as it battled Heracles. Its intervention caused the hero some inconvenience and a bitten foot, but was to no avail. Crushed under Heracles' boot, the crab was subsequently honoured with a place in the constellations by Hera.

The term 'dragon' conjures up images of scaled, flying reptiles to most people, but in Greek mythology it could be applied to any creature with serpentine characteristics. One such was Campe, a monstrous goddess with the body of a woman and the tail of a dragon or huge serpent, who had a scorpion-like stinger growing out of her back. She was assigned by the Titan Chronos to guard Tartarus and prevent the escape of the Hecatoncheires

THE CERYNEIAN HIND

Some creatures, such as the Ceryneian Hind, had a convoluted history. This story began when the nymph Taygete asked for help in avoiding the amorous attentions of Zeus. Artemis turned her into an animal, enabling her to hide from Zeus. By way of repayment, the nymph gifted Artemis with five hinds. The origins of these deer remain mysterious, but they were sufficiently magical that Artemis put four of them to work pulling her chariot.

The fifth hind escaped and ran loose in the hills of Ceryneia. Heracles was sent to capture it as one of his labours, which angered Artemis. However, the hero was able to convince Artemis not to punish him, as he intended to release the animal once he had fulfilled his end of the bargain. This in turn required some quick thinking, as the instigator of the labours, King Eurystheus, preferred to keep it. In the end the hind was released and continued to run wild.

and Cyclopes who he had imprisoned there. Campe carried out this task until slain by Zeus as he sought allies at the beginning of the Titanomachy.

Animals were associated with many of the gods. Some were mundane creatures sacred to a particular deity; others were more special. The Caucasian Eagle was a servant of Zeus, and may have been an automaton made by Hephaestus or a monstrous child of Echidna. The eagle was sent to snatch Ganymede from the mortal realm in order to serve as a cup-bearer in Olympus, and was the tormentor of Prometheus after he was chained for stealing fire. The eagle was eventually slain by Heracles.

Hyperborea

Far to the north of Greece and the other known lands lay the Rhipaion Mountains, home of the god Boreas, the north wind. These may have been what are now known as the Carpathians. Within the mountains dwelt a one-eyed people called the Arimaspoi, who were engaged in an ages-long struggle with the griffins: half-lion, half-eagle creatures that hoarded gold that the Arimaspoi treasured.

To the south of the mountains was Pterophoros, a land of eternal winter, while to the north was the rather more pleasant Hyperborea. Watered by the river Eridanos, which flowed south from the world-river of Okeanos into the heart of the land, Hyperborea was known as the Garden of Apollo, and brought forth two crops per year. It was ruled by three priests of Apollo, all of whom were descended from the god Boreas.

Perseus and later Heracles visited Hyperborea in the course of their quests, but the earliest mention of Hyperborea

THE WORLD OF GODS AND MORTALS

ABOVE: Phaethon's brief escapade in his father's sun-chariot caused immense damage and altered the landscape of North Africa. Only the timely intervention of Zeus prevented further tragedy.

is a story in which Phaethon, a son of Helios, asked to drive the god's chariot. Lacking his father's skill, Phaethon soon lost control of the chariot, causing the sun to lurch all about the sky. Before any of the gods could intervene, Phaethon accidently scorched North Africa, turned the lush plains to desert, and burned the skin of the people there black.

Before any greater destruction could be wrought, Zeus hurled his thunderbolt and struck the sun-chariot from the sky. It crashed in the river Eridanos, in Hyperborea. Phaethon was elevated to the heavens afterwards, either as a star or a planet depending on the version of the myth; his nymph-sisters, the Heliades, were transformed into poplar trees as they grieved for Phaethon.

People from Hyperborea feature in some myths, notably as pilgrims who set up shrines in Greece. These included the oracle at Delphi, though apparently the pilgrimage was very dangerous and the Hyperboreans eventually began making their sacrifices closer to home.

OPPOSITE: Tales of how the distant Arimaspoi people battled griffins for their gold were sufficiently well known to be incorporated in Ancient Greek art, ensuring that they survived into modern times.

North Africa and Beyond

The Ancient Greeks were familiar with parts of the North African coast, but what lay inland was the subject of myth and distorted travellers' tales. The deserts of North Africa, created when Phaethon lost control of his father's sun-chariot, were a barrier to exploration even if the maritime-orientated Greeks were inclined to push inland.

According to myth, the Atlas Mountains of western North Africa were home to satyr-like creatures. These may have been the result of distorted accounts brought home by travellers who encountered baboons. This land was also home to many strange creatures such as the dog-headed Kynokepaloi and the Blemmai, or Sternopthalmoi. These truly bizarre creatures had no head at all; instead, their eyes and other facial features were on their chest. It is difficult to deduce where these stories originated.

A tribe called the Makhlyes was said to live in the region known as Libya to the Ancient Greeks (this could refer to much of North Africa). They were hermaphroditic humans, male on one side of their bodies and female on the other. Close to them lived the Auseans, who worshipped Athena and celebrated their goddess by having their young women fight to the death with clubs. The fairest among the winning group was armed in Greek style and driven around in a chariot to celebrate.

Other tribes of Africa were thought to be equally fearsome. Legends spoke of tribes who hunted and ate only the greatest of predators, and of cannibals who ate only the flesh of humans. Some Roman sources appear to cite what they claim are Greek stories about the inhabitants of these regions. It is not certain whether these tales were of Greek origin, however.

Beyond the Pillars of Hercules lay the Atlantic Ocean, which was known to have islands that

BELOW: Perhaps having their origins in distorted accounts related by travellers, tales of strange almost-human people around the fringes of the known world were common. The Panotioi and the Pandai were both reputed to have immense ears on an otherwise human frame.

could be reached by a Greek vessel. According to legend, some of these islands were home to the Gorgades. This was a tribe whose women were entirely covered in hair; a myth that almost certainly originated with sightings of the many species of ape native to the region. Another tribe, named the Hippopodes as they were men with the feet of horses, was said to live on islands off the north coast of Scythia. These 'islands' may have been in the Baltic or actually part of Scandinavia.

Also dwelling in these cold northern lands were the Panotioi, who were men with huge ears that they could use as shelters from the cold. According to some stories, they could fly by flapping their ears. Giant-eared and dog-headed people were also said to live in India, along with the Nuloi. These strange people had feet that faced backwards, with eight toes on each of them. A similar group, the Abarimones, dwelled in the Himalayas.

At the very southern edges of the world lived tribes of pygmies who were at war with flocks of cranes. They were said to dwell in the outermost reaches of India and Africa. The Sciapods also lived in the same regions; they were humans with a giant foot on their single leg, who sheltered from the sun by lying in its shade.

It is not certain whether all of these legendary creatures were thought to exist by the Ancient Greeks, or whether they were inventions intended to make some point or provide a humorous moment in an otherwise rather grim tale of gods and mortals. Some are recorded by Roman writers who claim the Greeks told tales of these creatures.

ABOVE: It is a common rule of thumb that the more distant a place, the more bizarre the stories of what goes on there. If centaurs lived in Thessaly, then there was no reason not to believe that pygmies battled cranes at the edges of the world.

Thule and the Northern Islands

Despite the fact that it was common belief that the world ended at the Pillars of Hercules, there were those willing to venture beyond in search of new lands. Of course, there was no sudden disaster awaiting just outside the Straits of Gibraltar, and Greek

ABOVE: The great Greek mariner Pytheas is said to have dared the northern oceans as far as the Arctic Circle. Even without mythological monsters, these waters were highly dangerous for a vessel of the era.

mariners were able to follow the African coast south or the Iberian peninsula north. Few would have considered sailing out of sight of land; those who tried it were undoubtedly lost.

Despite this, explorers such as Pytheas ventured around the outer coasts and brought back information about what they found. Pytheas was born around 380BC. He was a native of Massilia, a Greek colony that is now Marseille. He is thought to have landed at various points on the coast, possibly in the British Isles, and may have conducted a circumnavigation of Britain.

Pytheas is said to have then continued north, finding a land he named Thule. There, he claimed, there was no night at the summer solstice, which suggests he might actually have been north of the Arctic Circle. Exactly where Thule lay is open to some conjecture; candidates include the Baltic islands, the Scandinavian mainland or even Iceland. Thule was considered to be the edge of the world, which to someone raised in the Mediterranean was not unreasonable. Conditions in the far north would have been quite beyond the experience of most Greeks, and might seem more like something out of myth than the natural world.

Astronomy and the Constellations

The Ancient Greeks took a scientific approach to explaining the movement of the stars and planets, but the constellations all had a mythological origin. The twelve constellations that moved on paths that intersected the dawn made up the zodiac, which is the same today.

Each of the signs of the zodiac was associated with one or more mythological stories, and some played an important role in the epic poems from which later generations derived much of their knowledge about Greek mythology. One such was Aries, the ram. When the children of the nymph Nephele were about to be sacrificed to the gods, she sent Krios Krysomallos to rescue them. This was a magical flying ram with a golden fleece, who was a child of Poseidon, and was rewarded for his efforts by being sacrificed to the gods. His fleece was placed in the grove of Ares – where it was later sought by Jason and his Argonauts – and Krios Krysomallos was placed in the heavens as the constellation of Aries.

BELOW: Jason was sent to carry out what seemed like an impossible task; to retrieve the Golden Fleece from the far end of the Black Sea. Actually getting the fleece was only a small part of the tale – the real challenge was reaching its resting-place.

The constellation of Taurus represents the Cretan Bull who fathered the minotaur and later caused havoc all over mainland Greece. It was finally slain by Theseus. Other creatures also gained a place among the stars after encountering heroes. Cancer was Karkinos, a valiant but ill-fated giant crab stomped to death as it tried to aid the Hydra in battle against Heracles. Likewise, Leo was the Nemean Lion slain by Heracles. It, too, was honoured by Hera by being made a constellation.

Among the other creatures honoured in the heavens was Skorpios, a giant scorpion sent to slay Orion. Originally, the constellation now known as Libra formed the claws of Skorpios.

There are multiple versions of the origins of the constellation Gemini. Some stories state that the constellation immortalizes two unrelated agricultural heroes, Iasion and Triptolemos, whose only real connection was that they had dealings of some sort with Demeter. More commonly, Gemini was held to be the twins Kastor and Polydeukes, whose legendary generosity earned them a place in the heavens. They were associated with horsemanship as well as travellers and hospitality.

ABOVE: The Dioscuri, Kastor and Polydeukes, are better known by their Romanized names Castor and Pollux.

Virgo was another deified figure, in this case the goddess Astraia, who represented justice and may be an aspect of Dike, one of the Horae. She dwelt among mortals on earth during the Golden Age, but the degeneration of humanity made the world unfit for her. By the Bronze Age there was so little justice left in the world that Astraia departed and took up her place in the heavens. The scales of the constellation Libra represented scales used by Themis, but were also associated with Astraia in this context.

Centaurus, now known as Sagittarius, was the wise centaur Kheiron. Like many other signs of the zodiac his demise was the work of Heracles, though in his case it was by accident. Wounded by an arrow poisoned with hydra blood, Kheiron gave up his immortality to be free of the pain and joined the stars of the zodiac.

Capricorn represented another creature made up of parts of others; in this case, a goat with the tail of a fish. This was the form chosen by Aigipan when he sought to escape from the monstrous Typhon. In some versions of the tale, Aigipan was able to assist Zeus by recovering his tendons after Typhon ripped them out. Typhon was also involved in some versions of the story of the constellation Pisces. The creatures depicted are either two fish who helped Aphrodite and Eros escape from Typhon, or the gods themselves in fish form. An alternative version states that the fish helped in the birth of Aphrodite.

Aquarius, the water-bearer, was originally the Trojan prince Ganymede, who was essentially kidnapped by Zeus to serve as a cup-bearer in Olympus. Why he of all the many gods and spirits was chosen to be so honoured remains unclear, though other figures from mythology were included in the non-zodiac constellations. These included Andromeda, who was rescued by Perseus, and her mother Cassiopeia.

Perseus himself is depicted among the stars, along with the great hunter Orion and the hero Heracles. Heracles' friend Pholus the centaur was given a place in the heavens, as was the dragon Ladon, whom he killed. The nymph Callisto, turned into a bear by a vengeful Artemis, is the constellation of Ursa Major. The river Eridanos in Hyperborea can also be found among the constellations.

BELOW: It is not at all clear why some heroes, creatures and gods were commemorated with constellations and others were not. Perseus and Heracles both have constellations, as does Orion, but Jason and Theseus do not.

OPPOSITE: **According to this entirely hypothetical map, Atlantis was separated from the Strait of Gibraltar by a fairly narrow strip of sea, hardly worthy of the name 'ocean'. Atlantis itself appears gigantic, on a par with Europe or perhaps even larger.**

There is no discernible pattern or scheme to the constellations; it appears that the Ancient Greeks simply named them for whatever object, person or creature came to mind at the time. These designations have survived almost unchanged to the present day, and since the stars themselves have moved very little since then, modern skies would be familiar to someone who lived in Homer's time.

Atlantis

The lost civilization of Atlantis does not appear in the early myths. Homer and Hesiod do not mention it, and there are no legends of heroes going there or events taking place in Atlantis. The first mention of this mysterious place is made by Plato in around 300BC, long after the commonly known Greek myths were written down.

It is probable that Plato himself did not believe Atlantis ever existed. In his work *Timaeus*, Atlantis is described by Critias, a real philosopher but used by Plato as a mouthpiece. Critias says he heard the story in Egypt and was assured of its veracity.

According to Plato by way of Critias, the lost civilization of Atlantis lay on an island in the Atlantic Ocean. Lying beyond the Pillars of Hercules, this island was described as being larger than Libya and Asia combined. By this, Plato meant that it had a greater land mass than everything that had been explored of North Africa plus part of Asia Minor, so this was really a continent rather than an island.

Plato states that the Atlantic Ocean was passable in those days by way of other islands, making it possible to reach a continent on the far side. The Ancient Greeks did not possess ships that could cross open seas; even in the relatively confined waters of the Mediterranean it was dangerous to venture out of sight of land. Thus Plato was describing a chain of islands right across the Atlantic Ocean, which would allow ships to island-hop their way across.

Atlantis is described by Plato as having been created by Poseidon, protected by rings of sea and land, with a fertile central area rich in metals. The Atlanteans could afford to cover their temple of great Poseidon with silver and to build

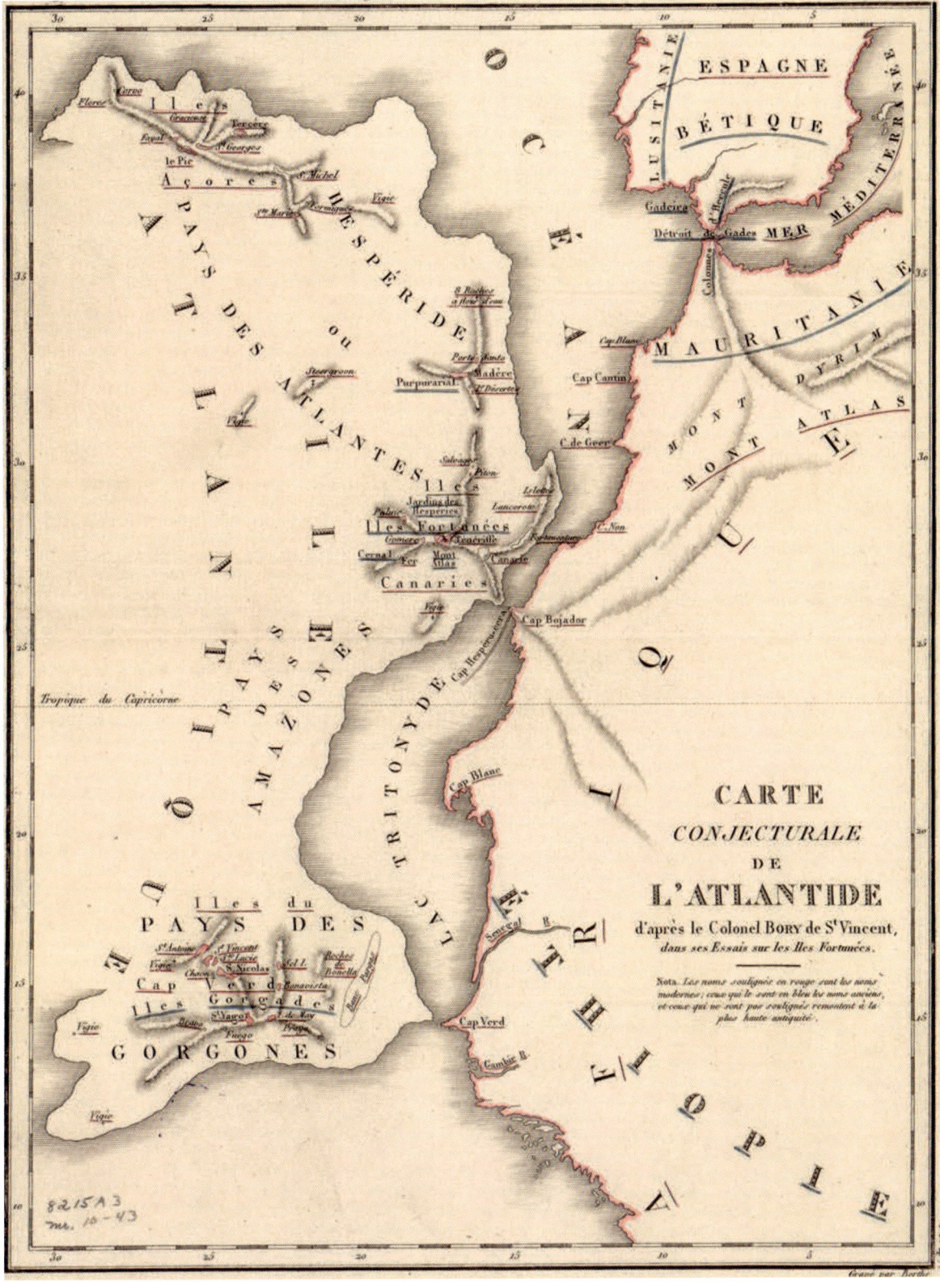

a wall of gold around their city. Their army could put 10,000 chariots into the field.

The powerful and advanced Atlantean civilization controlled land on the far continent and many islands in the Atlantic, and also had territory within the Mediterranean world. This extended across what the Greeks called Libya (North Africa) as far as the Nile and western Europe from the Atlantic coast to Italy. Not content with this, the Atlanteans decided they would push westward and conquer the rest of the world.

Around 9000 years before Plato's time of writing (and therefore around 6500 years before the first known settlement in Athens), the city led a defence against the advance of the Atlanteans, and ultimately stood alone against their power. By some means not recorded by Plato, Athens managed to defeat Atlantis and free all the people living within the Pillars of Hercules. Atlantis was later destroyed by violent earthquakes and sank beneath the sea, which made the Atlantic Ocean unnavigable in Plato's time.

Atlantis in popular culture
In a later work, *Critias*, Plato returns to the idea of all-powerful Atlantis being defeated by plucky little Athens. He states that the Atlanteans, despite being favoured by the gods, were overly enamoured of material things. They were greedy for wealth and personal power, and this offended Zeus, who decided to destroy them to make way for more law-abiding, prudent and harmonious people. There is no record of how Athens came to defeat the armies of Atlantis, as the remainder of the manuscript has not survived, but presumably Zeus and the Olympians aided their favoured people in some way.

This attitude seems to be somewhat at odds with Zeus' usual nature as a jealous and prideful god, but it does suit Plato's political agenda. Indeed, the whole Atlantis story seems to have been invented for the purpose of making a philosophical point. There are parallels to real places and events here and there, however, which has caused some people to look for a 'real' Atlantis.

The idea of a lost civilization in the middle of the Atlantic is used by some to 'prove' the existence of a culture that spanned

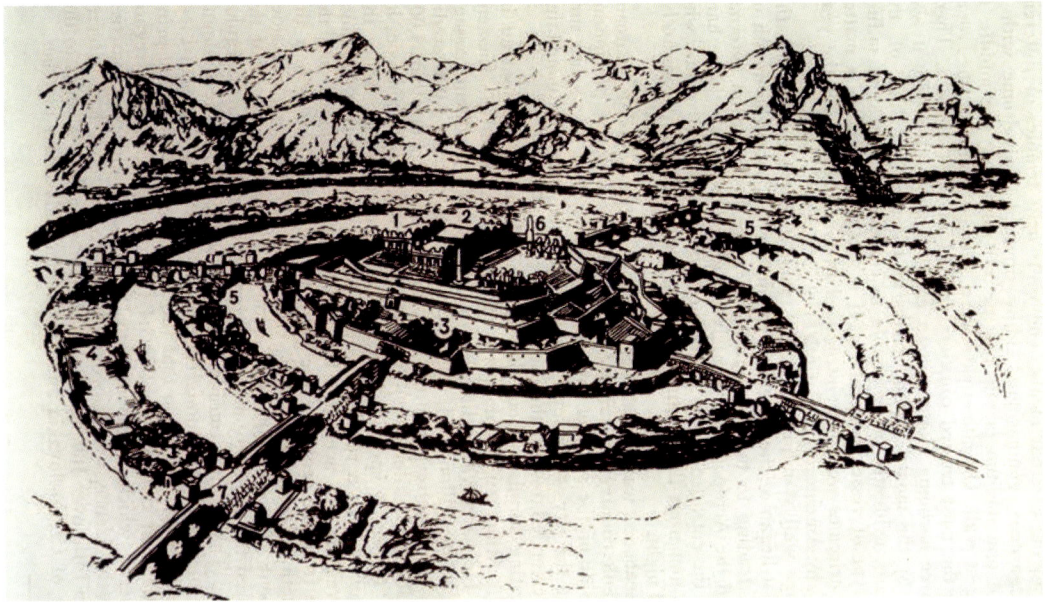

ABOVE: **Plato's description of Atlantis is of a fabulous place, with wealthy and powerful people dwelling amid the wonders they built. Their only weakness seems to have been a failure to follow Plato's social philosophy.**

the globe in very ancient times. This concept ties in with the – largely imaginary – similarities between pyramids built in Egypt, Asia and the Americas. Vaguely similar myths and gods are sometimes taken as further evidence that there must have been some pan-global civilization. However, the reality is that there is no good evidence of communication between the two sides of the Atlantic, and many reasons to believe there was none.

It is possible that Plato borrowed ideas from history. The defence of Greece against the extremely powerful Persian Empire and the destruction of the Minoan civilization – possibly connected to earthquakes and volcanic eruptions – may have been an inspiration for his tale, or perhaps Plato's Atlantis story was a distorted version of history. The most likely explanation is that Plato simply made it up.

This has not prevented the idea of Atlantis from passing into the common imagination. Modern finds of submerged cities are often dubbed 'the real Atlantis', and the wondrous civilization has been the subject of many works of fiction. However, it is probable that Atlantis was not part of the accepted mythical geography of the Ancient Greeks. No heroes had adventures there; no gods seduced or murdered mortals. Alluring as the legend of Atlantis may be, it is not really a part of mainstream Ancient Greek mythology.

5

HEROES AND WAR

Much of what we know about Greek mythology comes from the tales of heroes. Those in turn may have been derived from oral histories dating back to the era before the Greek Dark Age.

How much of any given tale is based on real events is open to question; the heroic legends are for the most part set in real places and in some cases there is evidence of conflict around the right time in history.

A city did exist where the Troy of Homer's *Iliad* is said to have stood, and it was destroyed by war in the time period Homer was writing about. This does not mean there was a Trojan horse, nor that gods took part in the fighting, but it does appear that the events of Homer's epic poem may be based on stories of a war that really happened. Similarly, some details of the hero-tales correspond to events known to have occurred.

OPPOSITE: **At the end of his career Heracles, greatest of the Greek heroes, ascended to Olympus and joined the ranks of the deities. His feud with Hera was finally put aside.**

Perseus

Perseus was the son of Danae, daughter of King Acrisius of Argos. Warned by an oracle that he would be slain by a son of Danae, Acrisius kept his daughter locked away in an underground prison made of bronze. This did not, however, stop Zeus from getting in – taking the form of a shower of golden rain – and impregnating Danae.

King Acrisius had Danae and her baby son, who was named Perseus, locked in a chest and thrown in the sea. Perhaps due to divine favour, they survived and were eventually snagged in the fishing nets of Dictys, brother of King Polydectes of Seriphos. Dictys sheltered Danae and her son in his home and hid them for long enough that Perseus was able to grow up, but eventually Polydectes found out about them and fell in love with Danae.

Having offered marriage and been rejected, Polydectes decided to coerce Danae, but first he needed to get rid of Perseus. He engineered a situation where Perseus needed to gift him with a horse, which the young man could not possibly afford. Perseus asked what other gift he could make instead and Polydectes told him to bring him the head of the Gorgon Medusa.

This seemed like a suicide mission – which was Polydectes' intention – but Perseus had no choice but to make the attempt. He was aided by Athena and Hermes, who loaned him a brightly polished shield and a sickle, and advised him to seek out the Graeae. These were three sisters of the Gorgons, who had one eye and one tooth between them. By holding these items hostage, Perseus forced the Graeae to reveal the location of the Gorgons' cave and the whereabouts of three other items he would need.

ABOVE: So fearful of the oracle's warning was Acrisius that he ordered his daughter Danae and her infant son set adrift in a chest. His cruelty set in motion the events that would ultimately lead to fulfilment of the prophecy.

Equipping himself with Hades' cap of invisibility, a set of winged sandals and a magical bag capable of holding Medusa's head, Perseus went to the cave of the Gorgons and found them asleep. Using Athena's brightly polished shield as a mirror, he was able to avoid looking at Medusa's face and being turned to stone by its hideous appearance.

LEFT: Setting an apparently impossible task for a hero in order to get rid of him was a common mistake in Greek legend. Perseus' slaying of Medusa gained him the perfect weapon with which to take his vengeance on Polydectes.

Perseus decapitated Medusa; from her neck sprang Pegasus the winged horse and the warrior Chrysaor. They presumably departed without incident, after which Perseus placed Medusa's severed head in his bag. He flew away on his winged sandals before the other two Gorgons awakened. Medusa's blood dripped from the bag and turned into serpents wherever it struck the ground.

As he made his way home, Perseus encountered Atlas and turned him to stone using Medusa's head, thus creating the Atlas Mountains of North Africa. He then reached the realm of King Cepheus, whose daughter Andromeda was to be sacrificed to a sea monster named Ketos. This came about because Cepheus' wife Cassiopeia had boasted she was more beautiful than the Nereids, thus angering the sea gods.

Accounts of how Perseus slew the sea monster vary. In some tales, he used the head of Medusa; in others he used the magical

BELOW: By slaying the sea-monster Ketos, Perseus thwarted the divine vengeance that was to be visited upon Andromeda for her mother's boasting. This might have had unfortunate consequences, but on this occasion the gods apparently accepted the situation.

sickle given to him by Hermes. Perseus and Andromeda were wed, and she accompanied him on his journey home. Upon arriving, he found that King Polydectes had been harassing his mother, and used Medusa's head to turn the king and his court to stone. After this, Perseus gave Medusa's head to Athena, who mounted it on her shield.

After returning his magical gifts to the gods, Perseus went in search of King Acrisius, eventually finding him attending the games at Larisa. Perseus decided to compete in the games, but accidentally hit Acrisius in the foot with his discus, killing him. Thus the king was indeed slain by a son of Danae.

Perseus apparently retired from the life of a hero, raising several sons with his wife Andromeda. He is credited with founding the city of Mycenae and was the father of a dynasty that included Perses, first king of Persia, and eventually Heracles.

ABOVE: Perseus is one of the few heroes who completed his task and settled down to a happy marriage. Among the descendants of Perseus and Andromeda was Heracles, who had a rather more troubled existence.

Cadmus

Cadmus is credited with introducing the alphabet to Greece. He was unusual among Greek heroes in that he was not a Greek but a Phoenician. The son of the king of Tyre, Cadmus left home with his brothers and his mother Telephassa to search for his sister Europa, who had gone missing. Unknown to her family, Europa had been seduced by Zeus in the form of a white bull, and carried off to Crete.

Eventually, Cadmus' brothers gave up their search and, since they had been commanded not to return without their sister, founded new cities where they took up residence. Cadmus and

Telephassa carried on, until she finally died in Thrace. Cadmus then sought guidance from the oracle at Delphi, which told him to follow a distinctive cow that was nearby and to found a city in that place. Cadmus did so, until the cow finally fell dead. He then sacrificed it to Athena and set about building a city on the spot.

Nearby was a spring sacred to Ares, from which a dragon emerged and attacked Cadmus' followers. He slew it and was instructed by Athena to sow half its teeth in the ground and give the rest to her. The teeth grew into supernatural warriors, who might have slain Cadmus. He tricked them by throwing stones so that they thought another of the warriors was attacking them. Confused, the warriors warred among themselves until only five remained. These helped Cadmus to build his city, which he named Thebes.

Ares was angry at the slaying of his dragon, and forced Cadmus to serve him for eight years, after which Cadmus was married to Ares' daughter Harmonia. Cadmus' long-lost sister Europa, now well established among the royalty of Crete, attended the wedding. However, despite finally locating his sister by this rather convoluted method, Cadmus had a miserable life. Among his misfortunes was the seduction of his daughter Semele by Zeus, resulting in her death when the god revealed his true form to her.

Cadmus eventually decided he would be less unhappy as a serpent. His wife Harmonia joined him in the transformation, which was made possible by the magic of the dragon Cadmus had slain. Zeus took pity on them and transferred Cadmus and Harmonia to Elysium.

Heracles

Heracles was the epitome of the superhuman warrior-adventurer. Roman writers called him Hercules, causing some confusion about exactly who performed certain great feats. The answer, of course, is that it was the same man.

Heracles was fathered by Zeus upon Alcmene, a mortal woman who was a descendant of the hero Perseus. This formidable parentage was the source of Heracles' strength and power, and also many of his troubles. Hera asked Zeus to bless the house of Perseus, so that the next child born to a member

HEROES AND WAR   163

ABOVE: The pregnancy of Alcmene was difficult due to the intervention of Hera, who slowed down the growth of the baby Heracles so that Zeus' blessing would be all upon Eurystheus instead.

would be a great king. Zeus readily agreed, since Alcmene was pregnant with Heracles, but Hera then slowed the pregnancy so that Heracles' cousin Eurystheus could be born first. This was by no means the last time Hera interfered in Heracles' destiny.

Despite this setback, Heracles got off to a good start in life. As a baby, he strangled two serpents that had been sent by Hera, who suspected that he was an illegitimate child of Zeus'. As he grew, Heracles was tutored by the most skilled individuals, including Kastor and Phanotes, a son of Hermes. Heracles learned the arts of the warriors, as well as literature and music. He excelled at everything and soon outshone his teachers.

As a young man, Heracles was sent by King Thespius after a lion that was killing cattle around Mount Cithaeron. After a long hunt, he killed it and took its hide. Some sources state that this was where Heracles got his trademark lion-skin cloak, although others say it was the hide of the Nemean Lion. On his way home, Heracles encountered the heralds of King Erginus of the Minyans, who were on their way to Thebes to collect tribute. Heracles cut off their ears, noses and hands and sent them back to their master.

This, unsurprisingly, caused a war that Heracles won, imposing a heavier tribute on King Erginus than Thebes had been required to pay. Upon his return, King Thespius decided his 50 daughters should each have a child by Heracles, and sent them to his bedchamber one by one. The grateful king of Thebes allowed Heracles to marry his daughter Megara. They had children too – sources vary as to how many – but Hera struck Heracles mad and he massacred them.

The Twelve Labours of Heracles: the first tasks
Seeking absolution, Heracles consulted the oracle, which told him to serve King Eurystheus and perform a series of tasks for him. These would become the Twelve Labours of Heracles, although originally there were only ten.

The first two were relatively straightforward monster slayings. The Nemean Lion had impenetrable skin and the Lernaean Hydra regrew its heads when they were cut off, but ultimately they were no match for Heracles' might. Thereafter, he wore the lion skin as a cloak and tipped his arrows in the Hydra's poisonous blood.

Heracles' third labour was different; he was instructed to capture the Ceryneian Hind, which was sacred to Artemis. King Eurystheus and Hera hoped the task would prove impossible or enrage the notoriously violent Artemis, but Heracles was able to capture the hind without harming it. Accounts vary; in some he used a net, in others he tripped the beast with an arrow between its feet as it ran. Some versions say that Artemis declared the task complete and told Heracles to let the hind go.

ABOVE: The Nemean Lion's skin was impervious to weapons, which had enabled it to kill all the previous warriors who came to slay it. Heracles solved the problem by strangling the beast.

The boar, the stables and the birds
For his next task, Heracles was told to capture the fearsome Erymanthean Boar. While searching for it, he encountered his friend Pholus, a centaur, and they shared some wine. Unfortunately, other centaurs arrived and became drunk, eventually attacking Heracles. He killed them with his poisoned arrows, accidentally wounding the great Kheiron in the process.

Kheiron was immortal and would have suffered forever, so he asked the gods to take away his immortality and allow him to replace Prometheus. This meant that Kheiron would suffer

BELOW: **Heracles risked the wrath of Zeus by slaying the eagle sent to torment Prometheus.**

RIGHT: **In addition to their formidable weaponry, the Stymphalian Birds were protected by a dangerous marsh. This enabled them to hide in their nests where hunters could not shoot them, but Heracles flushed them out with a rattle provided by Athena.**

Prometheus' torment instead, daily having his liver pecked out by the Caucasian Eagle. Heracles put a stop to this by killing the eagle. In some versions of the tale, Heracles freed Prometheus without the intervention of Kheiron.

The boar proved easy to catch once Heracles tricked it into venturing into deep snow. He brought it back to King Eurystheus, who was terrified of it. The boar may have been added to the king's menagerie, but in any case Heracles was given a new task. The stables of King Augeas were filled with magically healthy cattle, and had not been cleaned in 30 years. Heracles was tasked with doing so, and the job had to be done in a single day.

Heracles' solution was to divert the rivers Alpheus and Peneus into the stables, which rinsed away three decades of dung. He had asked for a tenth of the cattle in payment, but King Augeas refused. Heracles made a legal challenge against this decision – an unusual action for a hero – but was banished from the kingdom. He killed Augeas and placed his son Phyleus on the throne.

All this was in vain. King Eurystheus decided that the task had not been completed properly since Heracles had used a river instead of doing it himself, and that slaying the Hydra was also invalid since Heracles had had assistance from his nephew Iolaus. In the meantime, Heracles was sent to kill the Stymphalian Birds. These magical creatures were made by Ares, and fed on humans. Heracles scared them from their hiding places with a rattle provided by Athena, then shot most of them. The surviving birds fled and were later encountered by the Argonauts.

The bull and the girdle
Capturing the Cretan Bull, the next task, proved easy enough, but Eurystheus was not pleased. He was frightened and hid from the animal, while Hera refused the sacrifice when Heracles offered it. The bull was released or escaped, and continued to cause mayhem around Marathon. In the meantime, Heracles was sent to steal a group of mares owned by King Diomedes of Thrace. They were fed on human flesh, and ate one of Heracles' companions. He fed Diomedes to the mares after defeating his army and brought the now-peaceable animals to Eurystheus.

The ninth task was to obtain the girdle of Hippolyta, queen of the Amazons, which had been a gift from her father Ares. This started out well enough; Hippolyta was willing to gift

LEFT: The fight between Heracles and Amazon queen Hippolyta resulted from a misunderstanding fostered by Heracles' old enemy Hera. Otherwise, obtaining Hippolyta's girdle would have been the easiest of Heracles' labours.

BELOW: **Having already journeyed the length of the Mediterranean to steal Geryon's cattle on the island of Erytheia, Heracles was required to journey all the way back there to obtain apples from the garden of the Hesperides.**

Heracles with the girdle rather than fight him. He suggested they dine together aboard his ship, at which point Hera went among the Amazons and told them Heracles intended to kidnap their queen. They attacked his ship and, thinking himself betrayed, Heracles killed Hippolyta.

After returning with the girdle, Heracles was sent to steal the cattle of the giant Geryon, who lived on the island of the Erytheia. Along the way, he became enraged by the heat of the sun and tried to shoot it with his bow. Rather than being offended, Helios decided to help Heracles and loaned him the golden bowl that he used to sail across the seas during the night. Reaching the island of Erytheia, Heracles slew Geryon's two-headed dog Orthrus and his herdsman before confronting the three-headed giant and killing him with an arrow. Some versions of the tale add in various trials on the way home with the cattle.

The final tasks

Having now completed ten tasks as expected, Heracles was informed that two of them were invalid and he must now obtain the golden apples from the Hesperides. According to some sources, they grew on the island of Erytheia; this must have annoyed Heracles, as he now had to repeat his journey to the far end of the Mediterranean. In some versions of the story, Heracles persuaded Atlas to get the apples for him, holding up the heavens in Atlas' place while he was gone. In others, the tree was guarded by the dragon Ladon, which Heracles slew.

The next task was to capture the three-headed hound Kerberos, brother of Orthrus. To do so, Heracles had to enter the underworld. There he encountered Perseus and Pirithous, who were trapped in magical chairs by Hades. Heracles was able to rescue Perseus but not Pirithous, and requested

permission from Hades to borrow Kerberos. Hades agreed, providing Heracles could subdue the hound without using weapons. He did so, and presented him to Eurystheus.

Eurystheus was again terrified of the creature, and decided he did not want any more monsters brought before him. He declared Heracles' labours complete. Heracles took Kerberos home and set out for new adventures, joining the Argonauts in their quest for the Golden Fleece.

Heracles had many other adventures, slaying giants and kings. He got into a fight with Apollo at one point, as a result of disrespecting the Oracle of Delphi. Zeus separated the two with a thunderbolt. He eventually met his end through the vengeance of Nessus, a centaur who attacked his wife Deianira. Heracles used his poisoned arrows, tainting the blood of Nessus, who convinced Deianira to keep his shirt and give it to Heracles if she suspected him of infidelity. In due course she did so, and the toxic blood poisoned him.

Heracles built his own funeral pyre and convinced his friend Poeas to light it, immolating himself and ascending to Olympus. There, he was raised to divine status and married Hebe, daughter of Hera. This finally ended the feud between the two.

ABOVE: Heracles' penchant for poisoned arrows was his final undoing. Long after he killed the centaur Nessus, his bloodstained shirt was still toxic to the touch. Hercules chose to die as had his friend Keiron rather than endure the torment he had visited upon others.

Jason and the Argonauts

Jason was the son of Aeson, king of Iolcos, and Alcimede. Unusually for a Greek hero, he did not have any gods in the immediate family. However, his father's half-brother Pelias did, having been fathered upon a mortal woman named Tyro by Poseidon. Tyro abandoned her twin sons Pelias and Nelus, leaving them to die on a mountainside. They were found by a herdsman and eventually returned home to overthrow Aeson.

Pelias banished his brother Nelus and imprisoned Aeson, but was worried about a prophecy that he would be killed by a man wearing one sandal. After ruling for some years, he organized the Olympic games, to be held in Iolcus, and there he encountered a man with one sandal. This was Jason, son of Aeson, who had been secretly sent away to prevent Pelias killing him as he had all Aeson's other children.

Jason had been tutored by the centaur Kheiron and was already a highly accomplished individual, but was not above minor mishaps. On the way to the games, Jason helped a woman cross the river Anaurus, although he lost a sandal in the process. The woman was Hera, who for once was not opposed to a hero. This was partly since Jason was not the product of her husband's infidelity, and partly because she hated Pelias for failing to properly honour her.

BELOW: Pelias promised Jason his kingdom if he succeeded in retrieving the Golden Fleece. He would have been wise to honour his bargain with the hero who accomplished such an incredible feat.

The beginning of the journey

Jason presented himself and announced his parentage, perhaps naively hoping that Pelias would simply hand over his throne. Pelias was not willing to do so, but he did recognize Jason as his nemesis. He asked Jason what he would do if he ever met the man who would slay him, and Jason replied that he would send him on a mission to obtain the Golden Fleece. This was an impossible task, since the fleece lay far off in Colchis and was guarded by a dragon. Pelias thus ordered Jason to fetch him the fleece, and in return he promised to give up the throne of Iolcos.

Jason commissioned a ship, which was named Argo. Some sources describe this 50-oared galley as the first ship ever to set out on the seas, but it is more commonly described as the best. Athena assisted by contributing a timber from the speaking oak of Dodona, which was to serve as a lookout and guardian during the voyage. To crew this marvellous vessel, Jason assembled a crew of the best and finest men, who became collectively known as the Argonauts.

According to some sources, the Argonauts elected Heracles as their leader; in a rare moment of humility, Heracles declined and said Jason should lead, as this was his mission. Among the heroes aboard *Argo* was Orpheus, a great musician, and the twins Kastor and Polydeukes. Atalanta, the huntress who slew the Calydonian Boar, was there, along with many others.

ABOVE: The *Argo* is sometimes described as the first of all ships. This is usually interpreted as meaning *Argo* was so good that it was as if there had been no ships before it rather than crediting Jason with inventing maritime travel.

Lemnos and the Doliones

The Argonauts' journey was difficult, and many of their troubles might be considered fallout from the jealousy of the gods. At Lemnos, their first landfall, they found that the women of the island had slain all their menfolk. This resulted from a curse sent by Aphrodite, which caused the women to stink horribly. The men of the island were repelled, and consoled themselves with concubines from Thrace. Their wives killed them for it.

The Argonauts were not repelled by the women of Lemnos, however, and fathered many children upon them. These, according to the story, became the race known as Minyans. Historically, the Minyans were possibly an ancient indigenous population or invaders from north of Greece who settled in some areas well before the Greek Dark Age. Mythically, they were

OPPOSITE: **Rather than allowing Jason and his Argonauts to slay the Harpyai, the gods negotiated by sending Iris with a message. If the Argonauts refrained from killing them, the Harpyai would leave King Phineas alone.**

connected with various legends, some of which conflict with that of the Argonauts. For example, Heracles, who according to this story was one of the founders of the race, fought an army of Minyans after he maimed their heralds near Thebes.

After their visit to Lemnos, the Argonauts made landfall in the land of the Doliones, in the Propontis, and were warmly received by King Cyzicus. While foraging for food, they were attacked by six-armed giants; Heracles killed many of them and the Argonauts drove off the rest. A storm blew the ship back on to the coast, where the Argonauts were mistaken for pirates by the local population. A fight broke out, in which Jason killed King Cyzicus; it was not until dawn broke that the mistake became apparent.

After holding a funeral for the dead, the Argonauts pushed on, until Heracles broke his oar. Along with his friend Hylas, he went ashore to seek timber for a new oar, and Hylas was charmed by a sea nymph. Hylas drowned attempting to reach the nymph, and Heracles decided to part company with the Argonauts.

King Amykos and King Phineus

In Bithynia, the Argonauts encountered King Amykos, who was a tremendous boxer. Polydeukes agreed to fight him and won, since he was the greatest fistfighter in all the cosmos. This angered the Bebryces, Amykos' tribe, and they attacked the Argonauts. After another massacre, the Argonauts sailed on to Salmydessus in Thrace. There, they encountered the unfortunate King Phineus.

Phineus had been blinded by the gods, although sources differ as to his offence. He was also tormented by the Harpyai, monstrous bird-women who stole his food and befouled what remained. The Argonauts drove off the Harpyai and might have killed them, but the goddess Iris, acting as a messenger from Olympus, told them that King Phineus would no longer be harassed by the creatures. In gratitude, he gave the Argonauts the location of Colchis, where the Golden Fleece was to be found, and warned them of their next challenge.

The Symplegades lay ahead, clashing rocks that would crush any ship that tried to pass through. Following the advice of Phineus, Jason released a dove to test the timing of the rocks.

As they recoiled from smashing together, the Argonauts hauled on their oars and dashed through. Some accounts mention assistance from Athena and damage to the ship, but ultimately the vessel was able to navigate the hazard and sail on.

Further adventures are mentioned in some versions of the tale. The navigator fell asleep and went overboard, sending the ship off course towards an island inhabited by violent Amazons. A wind sent by Zeus to carry *Argo* away from the hazard instead blew it to the island where the Stymphalian Birds had taken up residence. They attacked the ship, but were driven off by the Argonauts clashing their weapons and shields to set up a frightening noise.

King Aeetes and Medea

Finally arriving at Colchis, Jason was told by King Aeetes, who ruled there, that he would give up the fleece if Jason performed a set of difficult tasks all in one day. The first was to plough a field

using the Khalkotauri, fire-breathing bulls. This seemed impossible, but Jason received assistance from an unexpected quarter.

Aeetes' daughter Medea was a priestess of Hecate, and knew sorcery. Hera persuaded Aphrodite to send Eros to her, causing Medea to fall in love with Jason. With the assistance of a magical salve that she prepared, Jason was protected from the bulls' fire and could plough the field as instructed. Next, Aeetes told Jason to sow dragon's teeth in the furrows he had ploughed. This was easy enough, but they sprouted into warriors. Like Cadmus, Jason solved this problem with misdirection. A well-placed stone caused some of the warriors to turn on others, and soon they were destroying themselves.

Since his tasks had not killed Jason, Aeetes decided on a more direct approach. He sent his men to slay the Argonauts, but led by Medea they slipped away to the sacred grove where the Fleece lay. There, Medea's sorcery and Orpheus' music caused the

LEFT: Jason's taming of the bulls of Aeetes demonstrates the reliance of Greek heroes on divine favour. Without the intervention of Aphrodite, Jason could not have obtained protection from the bulls' fire.

dragon guarding the Golden Fleece to fall asleep. Jason retrieved the Fleece and the Argonauts retreated swiftly to their vessel.

Aeetes pursued the Argonauts, but Medea killed her brother Apsyrtus using magic and scattered his pieces in the sea. Aeetes slowed his pursuit to gather the parts of his son, and the Argonauts escaped. However, Medea's actions had angered Zeus, who sent the *Argo* off course with storms.

The Argonauts were first driven close to the island where the Sirens dwelt, and might have been lured to their deaths by the Sirens' call had not Orpheus drowned out their music with his own. Then the *Argo* had to pass between the monsters Scylla and Kharybdis. Since they are normally said to lie in the straits between Sicily and Italy, it is clear that Zeus' storms had sent the Argonauts very far off course.

Guided by Thetis, who was acting on the instructions of Hera, the Argonauts threaded the correct path between the whirlpool and the six-headed monster, escaping destruction for the time being. Then, passing Crete, they were bombarded with stones by Talos, a giant man of bronze. Medea found his weakness; a vent that would cause his magical blood to drain out. Her spell removed the plug from this vent – possibly by hurling a rock against his ankle, where the vent lay – and Talos was slain.

After the journey
Returning home, Jason presented the Golden Fleece to Pelias and demanded his father's release from imprisonment. Pelias had murdered Aeson some time earlier, however, and was not willing to give up his kingdom. Medea was the instrument of Jason's vengeance; she tricked Pelias' daughters into thinking they could restore his youth by cutting him into pieces and boiling the remains.

Other versions of the tale state that Aeson was still alive but very old, and was restored to youth by Medea using some of Jason's blood. Pelias' daughters asked her to similarly rejuvenate Pelias, but Medea performed only part of the ritual. She cut Pelias' throat but did not replace his blood once it had spilled out.

Pelias' son Acastus exiled Jason and Medea immediately upon ascending to the throne. They went to Corinth, where Jason fell in love with another woman, who Medea murdered with a poisoned dress and coronet. She also slew the two sons she had borne to Jason and was taken to Athens by a chariot sent by her grandfather, the god Helios.

Medea married the king of Athens, Aegeus, and subsequently tried to kill Theseus when he presented himself at court. In some versions of the tale, she later returned to Colchis; in others she travelled east and ended her days in what is now Iran. Jason committed suicide in some versions of the story; in others he eventually managed to reclaim his father's throne but was no longer favoured by Hera, who did not like unfaithful husbands. He was eventually killed by a piece of the rotting *Argo*, which fell on him while he slept, a lonely old man, beneath its stern.

BELOW: Medea was a powerful and murderous woman, who carved out a place for herself at the court of Athens. Seeing Theseus as a threat to her position she responded the only way she knew how.

An early fight

One of Theseus' early fights was with Heracles' cloak, made out of the skin of the Nemean Lion. The other children of the palace fled when they saw the cloak where Heracles had put it down upon arriving, but Theseus attacked it thinking it was a real lion. The cloak came to no harm, but the incident was a portent of things to come.

Theseus

Theseus, like many Greek heroes, had a mix of godly and mortal parents and was conceived in questionable circumstances. His story began when King Aegeus of Athens journeyed to the oracle of Delphi to ask whether he would have any children, since neither of his wives had produced any. He received a rather confusing answer that amounted to advice not to drink wine before he got back to Athens.

Aegeus stopped on the way home to ask King Pittheus of Troezen what he thought the advice meant. Pittheus understood, and set about getting his guest drunk before introducing him to Pittheus' daughter Aethra. The two spent the night together, and later that night Poseidon also visited Aethra. Theseus was the child of this union, though whether Poseidon, Aegeus or both should be considered his father remains an open question.

When Theseus came of age, his mother told him that King Aegeus had left his sword and sandals under a giant rock. If a child resulted from their union, and that child was exceptional enough to be able to lift the rock, he should take the items to Athens as a token of his parentage.

Along the way, Theseus encountered a warrior named Periphetes, who was in the habit of savagely clubbing those he encountered. Theseus took his club away and, after slaying Periphetes with it, decided he would keep it for his own. He dispensed poetic justice to several other opponents along the way: Cercyon the wrestler was wrestled to death and Sciron, who liked to kick people off a cliff for a giant turtle to eat, was fed to the turtle. Theseus also slew the Crommyonian Sow, a giant pig whose equally monstrous offspring was the subject of the Calydonian Boar Hunt.

Theseus and the Minotaur

Arriving in Athens, Theseus ran afoul of Medea, a sorceress and former lover of Jason who was King Aegeus' latest wife. She plotted against Theseus, as she did not want someone else's son inheriting the kingdom, and arranged for Theseus to be sent to deal with the Marathonian Bull. This was the same bull that had terrorized Crete and fathered the Minotaur there, and that had been captured by Heracles but had escaped or been turned loose again.

Theseus killed the bull and offered it as a sacrifice, at which point Medea tried to poison him at a feast. He was saved when King Aegeus recognized his own sword and sandals, and realized what was happening. Honoured and made heir to the kingdom, Theseus soon came to realize he had inherited a problem.

Athens at the time was forced to pay tribute in the form of young men and women to King Minos of Crete, to be sacrificed to the Minotaur. Theseus volunteered to be one of the sacrifices, intending to slay the Minotaur rather than being eaten by it. Upon arriving in Crete he won the affection of Ariadne, daughter of King Minos. Ariadne provided a ball of thread to help Theseus find his way back out of the labyrinth, and with it he was able to return safely after locating and killing the Minotaur.

Theseus was married to Ariadne almost immediately and the tribute requirement was revoked; presumably King Minos did not feel it was wise to argue with someone who had just clubbed his Minotaur to death. The marriage was short-lived; Theseus

LEFT: **In addition to divine favour, powerful women were also vital to the success of Greek heroes. In Theseus' case it was Ariadne, daughter of King Minos, who helped him find his way through the labyrinth housing the Minotaur.**

abandoned Ariadne on the island of Naxos, although some versions of the tale state that he was forced to do so because Dionysus wanted Ariadne for his wife.

Theseus' return

Theseus returned home, but apparently forgot about the prearranged signal his father Aegeus was expecting. The agreement was that if Theseus was dead, slain by the Minotaur, the ship's sail would be black. If he won the fight he would fly white sails. Unaccountably, his vessel approached Athens with a black sail and Aegeus threw himself off the high place where he had climbed to watch for his son's return.

Theseus thus inherited the kingdom of Athens, and raised it to greatness by his deeds as a warrior. After unifying Attica under his rule, he campaigned against the Amazons and brought their queen to Athens to be his wife. He later married Ariadne's sister Phaedra, who subsequently fell in love with Hippolytus, Theseus' son by his Amazon wife. When Hippolytus rejected her advances, she claimed he had tried to rape her. Theseus cursed his innocent son, who was subsequently killed, and Phaedra committed suicide.

Theseus subsequently had to be rescued from the realm of Hades by Heracles, who happened to be passing on an unrelated

RIGHT: Theseus' tale was not a happy one. Spurned by her stepson Hippolytus, Theseus' wife Phaedra engineered his downfall and, in so doing, her own. Thereafter, Theseus suffered further misfortunes and was eventually murdered.

quest. Theseus and his friend Pirithous had come up with the questionable idea of entering Hades' realm and abducting Persephone. Theseus was rescued, but Pirithous was trapped in the underworld. However, upon his return to Athens, Theseus found his throne had been usurped by Menestheus with the assistance of Kastor and Polydeukes. Seeking refuge with King Lycomedes of Scyros, Theseus was betrayed and shoved off a cliff to fall to his death.

The Trojan War

The tale of the Trojan War is told by Homer in his epic poem the *Iliad*, which is considered to be the oldest work of Western literature. It may be that Homer simply recorded an earlier oral tradition, or he may have embellished one. Little is known for sure about the poet himself, but the *Iliad* contains many elements found in subsequent heroic fiction. In many ways it is the archetype of the heroic adventure story.

The causes of the Trojan War were complex, and as usual the gods were at fault. Zeus had been warned that the nymph Thetis would bear a son who surpassed his father, which was undesirable if she took a husband or lover among the gods. The solution was to marry her to a mortal, and Zeus chose King Peleus. Peleus was king of the Myrmidons, a legendary people native to Thessaly who were created by Zeus out of a colony of ants.

Peleus had a questionable past including murders and accidental homicide, but he does appear to have been a formidable warrior. Zeus instructed him on how to capture Thetis and force himself upon her, after which a wedding took place. This was to be attended by all the gods except Eris, goddess of discord, who was excluded to avoid trouble at what was more than likely a tense occasion.

Eris forced her way into the wedding anyway, armed with a golden apple that may have been from the tree given to Hera upon her wedding to Zeus. Eris threw the apple into the wedding, declaring it was for the fairest of all goddesses; immediately, Hera, Aphrodite and Athena began arguing over who should have it. Zeus was asked to provide judgement but wisely declined, giving the task to King Paris of Troy.

Paris and Helen

The three goddesses attempted to bribe Paris, but it was Aphrodite who was successful. She gave Paris the ability to seduce any woman, which he used on Helen, wife of King Menelaus of Sparta. Helen was well connected; she was a daughter of Zeus and her sister Clytemnestra was married to King Agamemnon of Mycenae. Despite the obvious dangers, Paris took Helen to Troy, where he would be under the protection of his father, King Priam.

The Greeks decided to launch an expedition to rescue Helen, and perhaps more importantly to avenge the insult they felt at her abduction. They were led by King Agamemnon of Argos, which was sometimes known as Mycenae. Agamemnon was married to Helen's sister Clytemnestra, and commanded a powerful force of warriors and ships. However, his expedition did not go well at first.

BELOW: The abduction of Helen, Queen of Sparta, sparked the conflict known as the Trojan Wars. Although most of Troy's subject cities were captured early in the war, Troy herself required a ten-year siege and only fell by trickery.

ABOVE: The Judgement of Paris illustrates the vanity and pettiness of the Greek gods. Hera, Athena and Aphrodite offered all manner of inducements to King Paris of Troy if he would name them fairest among the goddesses.

Having offended Artemis, Agamemnon was beset by unfavourable winds and storms that prevented his fleet from even setting out. Artemis demanded the sacrifice of Agamemnon's daughter Iphigenia in redress. In some versions of the tale Iphigenia was killed; in others Artemis accepted a deer instead, possibly taking Iphigenia into her service.

The siege of Troy

Despite the capture of several cities, the campaign against Troy did not result in the hoped-for quick victory, instead becoming bogged down in a siege lasting ten years. Homer's *Iliad* takes place at this point in the war, with the Greeks camped around Troy and the fighting locked in stalemate. Achilles was present with the Greek army, wearing the armour of his father Peleus, who was too old to take part in the war, and leading his warriors, known as Myrmidons.

The Greek cause was undone by bickering among their leaders. Achilles had captured a Trojan woman named Chryseis, whose father was a priest of Apollo. When Agamemnon refused

ABOVE: The Greek kings and heroes were also prone to childish squabbles according to Homer. Agamemnon's act of spite towards Achilles, after being forced to return Chryseis to her father, fragmented the Greek army.

to return Chryseis to her father, the Greek camp was struck by a plague. Achilles and other Greek leaders persuaded Agamemnon to release Chryseis, but in retaliation Agamemnon took Briseis, Achilles' prize, from him.

Achilles refused to take any further part in the war and pulled his Myrmidons out of the fight as well, weakening the Greek cause. Some leaders wanted to abandon the siege, but Odysseus persuaded them to fight on. A brief truce then ensued, during which King Menelaus of Sparta challenged Paris of Troy to single combat. The prize was to be the return – or not – of Menelaus' wife Helen.

Menelaus was a more accomplished warrior than Paris, and soon had the better of him. However, Paris had the support of Aphrodite, who rescued him and brought him safely back within the walls of Troy. Meanwhile, Athena, possibly at the urging of Hera, convinced the archer Pandarus – who was fighting for Troy – to try to assassinate Menelaus. Pandarus took the shot, but Athena deflected the arrow so that Menelaus was only wounded. This was enough to cause the truce to break down without greatly harming the Greek cause.

The hero Diomedes

As the fighting was renewed, the Greek hero Diomedes distinguished himself in combat, killing many Trojan warriors. Pandarus tried to bring his rampage to an end, but again his arrow was deflected by Athena, and almost immediately he was slain by a spear thrown by Diomedes.

Diomedes had made his name as one of the Epigoni. These were the sons of seven warriors – known as the Seven Against Thebes – who had tried to overthrow King Eteocles of

Thebes. The Epigoni succeeded where their fathers had failed, establishing Diomedes' reputation as a fearsome warrior.

In addition to commanding the second-largest Greek contingent in the war, Diomedes was equipped with magical armour, which may have been made by Hephaestus, and was favoured by Athena, who caused fire to erupt from his shield and helmet. During the battle he found himself facing the Trojan hero Aeneas, whose hip he crushed with a large rock. Aeneas' mother, Aphrodite, tried to rescue him, but Diomedes wounded her and drove her off, making him only one of two mortals to harm a god (Heracles was the other).

Apollo then attempted to aid Aeneas, and Diomedes – ignoring the advice of Athena – attacked him. Apollo warned Diomedes off, then asked Ares, god of battle, to take the field on the Trojan side. The Greeks pulled back in the face of his onslaught, but Athena came to Diomedes' aid. Using the helmet of Hades to make her invisible, she joined him in his chariot and together they launched an attack on Ares.

Ares threw his spear at Diomedes but Athena, whose presence he did not suspect, deflected it. She guided Diomedes' return blow, sorely wounding Ares, who fled the field. Having wounded two gods in a single battle, Diomedes might have fallen victim to excessive pride, but he did not, and indeed announced that he would not fight any more immortals when he was confronted by the warrior Glaucus.

After establishing that Glaucus, who was a descendant of Bellerophon, was not a god in disguise, Diomedes engaged him in conversation and the two established that their ancestors had been friends. They agreed not to fight one another, but Diomedes did put himself forward when the Trojan Hector offered single combat.

ABOVE: After wounding Aphrodite when she tried to help her son Aeneas, Diomedes tried to take on Apollo, and succeeded – with Athena's help – in wounding Ares and driving the god of war from the battlefield.

Hector and Achilles

Several other warriors put themselves forward, and in the end Ajax faced Hector. He survived, and after their encounter they exchanged gifts. Zeus at this point had forbidden the gods from further involvement but was assisting the Trojan cause. Together with the absence of Achilles, this caused the tide to turn against the Greeks.

Diomedes and Odysseus attempted to restore the situation by making a stealthy night raid on the Trojan forces, but this could not prevent further Trojan successes. With the Greeks' ships under threat of attack and Agamemnon, Diomedes and Odysseus all wounded, the Greeks begged Achilles to help them. Still he would not, although he sent his lover Patroclus out to lead the Myrmidons back into the fight.

Patroclus was dressed in Achilles' armour, and was mistaken for Achilles by Hector. With the aid of Apollo, Hector slew Patroclus, driving Achilles into a rage. Finally taking the field and equipped with armour fashioned by Hephaestus, Achilles slew Hector and dragged his body behind his chariot, by the belt Hector had received from Ajax.

BELOW: Achilles mourned his lover Patroclus, as well he might. Achilles' refusal to fight for the Greek cause forced Patroclus to impersonate him, resulting in a mismatched fight with Hector that could have only one outcome.

The *Iliad* ended with the slaying and funeral of Hector, although there are some associated stories. One concerned the death of Achilles, who was killed by an arrow shot by Hector's brother Paris. Guided by Apollo, the arrow struck Achilles in his only vulnerable spot, his heel. This was where his mother Thetis had held him as she dipped him in the river Styx to make him invulnerable.

Odysseus and Ajax retrieved the body of Achilles, and quarrelled over who would receive the arms and armour of the fallen warrior. Accounts of how this was settled vary, but in the end Odysseus was given the honour. This caused Ajax to go mad with rage and start attacking his comrades. Some versions of the tale state that Athena caused him to see Greeks where there were only cattle, and after he recovered his senses Ajax was mortified to see he had massacred defenceless cows. He fell on the sword that Hector had gifted him, killing himself.

The end of the war

Eventually the war was won by deception. The Greeks feigned retreat, leaving behind a giant wooden horse as a gift for the Trojans. This was a ruse devised by Odysseus, enabling a force of Greeks to hide inside and be taken inside the Trojans' defences. Cassandra, daughter of King Priam and sister to Paris and Hector, warned against taking the horse inside the walls, but she had been cursed by Apollo so that her prophecies were never believed.

The Trojan horse enabled the Greeks to launch a surprise attack and finally break Trojan resistance. The fall of Troy was accompanied by great violence and destruction, and several temples were sacked, which angered the gods. As a result, most of the participants had a very difficult journey home, and in many cases found a troubled household when they arrived. Agamemnon and Diomedes found their wives had been unfaithful, which may have been attributed to the fact that Aphrodite was fighting for the opposing side.

Idomeneus, commander of the Cretan contingent, offered to sacrifice to Poseidon the first living thing he saw upon landfall if the sea god would spare his ship during a storm. This turned out to be his son, and Idomeneus reluctantly kept his word.

ABOVE: The siege of Troy was brought to an end the famous ruse of the Trojan Horse. In their triumph the Greeks sacked the temples of many gods and brought disaster upon themselves.

This kin-slaying angered the gods, who struck Crete with a plague. This incident, as much as any other, sums up the relationship the Greeks had with their gods.

The *Odyssey*

The *Odyssey* is a sequel to the *Iliad*, also written by Homer. Unlike the *Iliad*, which features a range of major characters, the *Odyssey* focuses on the attempt by Odysseus to return home to Ithaca after the end of the Trojan War. Other sequels were created by Greek writers but are now lost, while some Roman writers added to the tradition with their works.

Odysseus was, like many Greek heroes, descended from the gods. His father sailed on the *Argo* with Jason, and his grandfather was a son of Hermes. Odysseus was a clever man, both wise and cunning, and a formidable war leader. In his youth he had been wounded by a boar during a hunt, in an incident that both proved his prowess and taught him that victory sometimes comes at great cost.

As a prince of Ithaca, Odysseus was one of the many suitors of Helen, who eventually married Menelaus of Sparta. Odysseus was more interested in Penelope, her cousin, and received support in his bid to marry her in return for brokering a deal among the suitors. There was a real chance of violence among some or all of them, but Odysseus got them to swear to respect Helen's final choice and to support the marriage.

Thus the marriage of Helen and Menelaus passed off peacefully, and Odysseus duly married Penelope. They were by all accounts happy together, and had one child, named Telemachus. When Helen was abducted by Paris of Troy, Odysseus did not want to take part in the resulting Trojan War. This was not least since he was aware of a prophecy that stated that his return home would be long delayed.

Odysseus in the Trojan War

The oath that had been Odysseus' own idea now compelled him to assist in the war. He tried to get out of it by feigning madness but Palamedes, who had been sent to recruit him for the endeavour, exposed the ruse. With no alternative, Odysseus joined the expedition. Since he had failed to avoid it, he had no sympathy for Achilles when he also tried to get out of taking part.

Achilles had been warned that he would either have a long and peaceful life or a short and glorious one, and was hiding on the island of Scyros disguised as a woman. Odysseus in turn had been informed that Achilles was essential to the Greek cause, and exposed the disguise.

In addition to recruiting Achilles and providing wise counsel to the Greek leaders, Odysseus performed deeds of courage and violence in the ten-year war against Troy. His greatest contribution was the idea of the Trojan horse, which enabled the Greeks to win the war, and during the conflict he took revenge upon Palamedes. He was also responsible for the death of Hector's baby son Astyanax.

ABOVE: **The blind seer Tiresias lived a very long life during which, according to some sources, he was transformed into a woman and, later, back again. He pronounced the future for many notables including Odysseus.**

Odysseus' long journey home

When the war was over, Odysseus began his journey back home to Ithaca. Almost immediately, his legendary wisdom failed him. His 12 ships were driven off course by unfavourable winds and landed in the territory of the Cicones, who were allies of Troy. Victorious in the ensuing fight, Odysseus' men spared a priest named Maron, who gave them wine. The warriors got drunk and were attacked by more forces of the Cicones, suffering serious casualties before they could withdraw to their ships.

More men were lost in the land of the lotus-eaters, though not to enemy action. Instead, the Greeks ate the lotus and wanted to stay. Odysseus managed to get his men back to their ships and sailed on, eventually reaching Sicily, which was the home of the Cyclopes. Trapped in a cave by the Cyclopes' leader Polyphemus, Odysseus blinded the giant with a stake, enabling his surviving followers to escape by hiding under the bellies of sheep.

Polyphemus was a son of Poseidon, who cursed Odysseus and his followers. This would have the effect of greatly prolonging the voyage, but in the meantime Odysseus and his companions came close to getting home. This was due to the assistance of Aeoleus, who had a bag containing the winds. He gave it to Odysseus, who left the other winds inside but allowed the gentle west wind to blow his ship homeward.

Odysseus' men decided that the bag must contain gold or other treasure and set about stealing it while he was asleep. This resulted in the winds being freed, blowing the expedition back to the island of Aeoleus. He refused to help Odysseus further, and a week after leaving his island 11 of the 12 ships were sunk by a tribe of giants named the Laestrygonians.

Reaching the island of Aeaea, the companions of Odysseus ventured ashore, but many of them were turned into pigs by the sorceress Circe who lived on the island. Protected by a herb given to him by Hermes, Odysseus resisted the sorceress' magic and confronted her. She became his lover and agreed to turn the warriors back into men.

Odysseus stayed on the island of Aeaea for a year, after which Circe helped him enter Hades to gain information. He learned of his wife's predicament at home in Ithaca. Penelope was surrounded by suitors who thought Odysseus dead, and was stalling them to give her husband time to get home. He was also forewarned about some of the dangers to come.

These warnings and the advice of Circe allowed Odysseus to get past the deadly Sirens. He ordered his men to block their ears with wax, rendering the Sirens' song ineffective, while he was lashed to the mast of his ship so that he could hear the song without being able to lead his men to their doom. Likewise, the ship managed to slip past Scylla and Kharybdis with only a handful of casualties. However, when Odysseus' men ignored his warning not to eat the sacred cattle of Helios on the island of Thrinacia, Zeus sent a storm that slew all of them save Odysseus.

Washed up on the shore of Ogygia, Odysseus became the captive of Calypso, whose magical song enthralled him for seven years. However, his desire to see his wife Penelope again eventually allowed him to break free with the help of Hermes and Zeus, and Odysseus continued his journey.

BELOW: **Odysseus had himself lashed to the mast of his ship so that he could hear the call of the sirens but not act upon it. Heeding good advice he was able to avoid many perils, but his crew were not so wise and all perished.**

OPPOSITE: The winged horse Pegasus provided a solution to most problems faced by the hero Bellerophon, enabling him to slay the Chimera while staying out of reach of its fiery breath.

Odysseus' return to Ithaca

Eventually Odysseus reached Ithaca, 20 years after he had left to fight in the Trojan Wars. He was well remembered by some of his people, and was reunited with his son Telemachus, who had been an infant when he left. Telemachus was now a warrior in his own right, and escaped an ambush laid by the suitors of Penelope to reach his father.

Odysseus returned home in disguise, and although he was recognized by his former wet-nurse, his identity was not revealed. His wife Penelope announced that she was ready to marry one of the suitors at last, and it would be whoever could string Odysseus' bow. Only Odysseus could do it, and with the weapon he slew all of the suitors. His identity was proven to Penelope by secrets about their home that only he would know.

In some versions of the tale, Odysseus and Penelope lived a long and happy life. In others, Odysseus was slain by Telegonus, his son by Circe. Either way, he does not appear to have had further adventures.

Bellerophon

Bellerophon is known today mainly for his association with the winged horse Pegasus and as a cautionary tale regarding hubris, or lack of humility. He was a son of Poseidon, though his ostensible father was King Glaucus of Corinth. Bellerophon desired to tame Pegasus, but could not catch the winged horse. Athena came to his assistance, sending him a dream about a golden bridle; when he awoke, Bellerophon had the bridle in his hands.

The bridle allowed Bellerophon to capture Pegasus, and soon afterwards he was granted permission to marry Aethra, daughter of King Pitheus. However, he was banished for killing a man – sources vary as to exactly whom – and eventually came to the court of King Proteus. There he was absolved of his crime but falsely accused of trying to seduce Proteus' wife Stheneboea.

The rules of hospitality meant that Proteus could not harm Bellerophon while he was a guest, so Proteus sent Bellerophon to the court of King Iobates with what was ostensibly a letter of introduction. In fact, the letter contained a request that Iobates kill Bellerophon, but it was not presented until the hero

was established as a guest and protected by the same rules that troubled Proteus.

Iobates came up with a win-win solution. He gave Bellerophon a set of tasks that would either get him killed or rid Iobates of some troubles. The first task was to slay the Chimera, a fire-breathing, three-headed monster. Some sources state that Bellerophon tamed Pegasus specifically to defeat the Chimera; his method varies too. In some tales, he flew out of reach of its fire and shot arrows at the beast, while in others he used a spear to deliver a block of lead into the monster's throat, causing it to choke on molten metal.

Next, Bellerophon was sent to make war on an entire tribe, the Solymi. After he defeated them, he was ordered to attack the Amazons. His tactic was to use Pegasus as an airborne archery platform, shooting from a height that archers on the ground could not reach. Even an ambush by Iobates' army proved ineffective, but it did reveal the king's intent.

However, Iobates had come to realize that Bellerophon was a very special man, and doubted he really had tried to seduce Stheneboea. He offered a reconciliation, granting Bellerophon half his kingdom and marriage to his daughter. Bellerophon accepted, but he had become excessively proud and thought he could ride Pegasus to Olympus itself. When he tried, Zeus sent a fly to sting Pegasus, who shied and threw Bellerophon off. Pegasus continued to Olympus where he was greatly honoured, while Bellerophon fell back to earth and ended his days as a blind cripple.

Notable Figures

Some of those who met an unusual fate or stood out from the masses of Greek citizenry were not heroes in the usual sense. Indeed, many were talented but unwise, or even just unfortunate. Among them was Arachne, a great weaver who felt that she could rival even the gods. She challenged Athena to a contest, and Athena produced a wondrous depiction of the noble and regal gods. Arachne, on the other hand, chose to depict the gods as animalistic, amid an orgy with mortal women. Athena was offended and delivered such a beating that Arachne hanged herself, after which Athena turned her into a spider.

Lykaon, King of Arkadia, also challenged the gods – in this case, Zeus. Lykaon had 50 sons, who were by all accounts rather bad characters. He decided to test Zeus' perception by serving his own son Nyctimus as a meal. Zeus did indeed notice, and turned Lykaon and his remaining sons into wolves as a punishment. In some versions of the tale, the sons were complicit in the creation of the meal and subsequently struck down by thunderbolts. In all cases, Nyctimus was restored to life or spared Zeus' wrath.

Virtually the same story is told about Pelops, after whom the Peloponnese was named. In this tale, it was King Tantalos who served his son – Pelops – at a feast to the gods. Pelops was returned to life minus his shoulder, which had been eaten by Demeter. He was given an ivory replacement upon his resurrection. Pelops went on to feature in other myths, deceitfully winning a chariot race by having King Oenomaus' charioteer sabotage his vehicle.

The king was killed as a result, and Pelops murdered the saboteur as well. This resulted in a curse that led to Pelops' descendants having more eventful lives than most mortals would want. Among them was Niobe, Queen of Thebes, who boasted that her many children made her better than Leto, who had only two. Those two children were Apollo and Artemis, however, and they evened the score by massacring Niobe's offspring.

BELOW: Apollo and Artemis, though generally portrayed as 'good' or positive gods, were so jealous and vengeful that they massacred the children of Niobe over what they considered to be a slight to their mother.

The myth of Sisyphus

Another mortal punished in Tartarus was Sisyphus, although there are several versions of how he offended the gods. In some tales he was clever enough to capture death when his time came to die, which was an affront to Hades and a great inconvenience to those troubled by the should-be-dead who remained on Earth. In others, Sisyphus annoyed Zeus by revealing to the river-god Asopus that Zeus had abducted Asopus' sister Aegina.

Sisyphus may also have cheated death again, this time by finding loopholes in the rules that governed the destination of the dead. Permitted to return to life for a while in order to correct discrepancies in his burial method, he broke his word and remained alive for many more years. For these crimes, Sisyphus was condemned to endlessly push a round boulder up a hill, only for it to roll down again when he got to the top. This cycle of endless, pointless labour resulted in an existence without hope.

In an alternate version of this story, King Tantalos offended the gods by trying to obtain their magical food and drink – ambrosia and nectar – for himself. He was punished by being forced to spend eternity standing in a stream in Tartarus. When he tried to drink, the waters receded; when he tried to reach up to grab fruit from the branches above his head they, too, moved beyond his reach.

Some characters appeared in the stories of others and gained a small myth of their own along the way. Among them was Daedalus, a facilitator of other people's adventures rather than a hero. A notable inventor and sculptor, he fled Athens after murdering his nephew. This may have been out of jealousy at the boy's talent. Be that as it may, Daedalus made his way to Crete, where he was employed by King Minos. One of his first tasks was to create a hollow cow so that Minos' queen Pasiphae could mate with the Cretan Bull. Daedalus then designed the labyrinth that would house the child of this union.

Daedalus provided the thread that Theseus used to find his way through the labyrinth. For this he was imprisoned there by King Minos, along with his son Icarus. Daedalus' plan to escape involved making wings out of feathers and wax. This worked well enough that Daedalus was able to fly to Sicily, but Icarus flew too close to the sun and the wax holding his feathers in place melted. When King Minos pursued Daedalus to Sicily he was killed by the daughters of the royal household.

Leda, Queen of Sparta, was one of Zeus' many mortal lovers. In this case he took the guise of a swan, causing Leda to lay eggs. Some versions of the tale have more than one egg, with various figures within them, but most agree that Kastor and Polydeukes

– known as Dioscuri for their divine parentage while they lived among mortals – were born from one of the eggs. Kastor and Polydeukes later travelled with the Argonauts and participated in the Calydonian Boar Hunt. Those myths that give them siblings name them as Helen and Clytemnestra, wives of kings who participated in the Trojan wars.

Psyche was another mortal who attracted divine displeasure. She was so beautiful that Aphrodite became jealous and ordered Eros to make her fall in love with the most unattractive man he could find. Eros accidentally scratched himself with one of his arrows and instead fell in love with Psyche. Eventually he abandoned her and she wandered the world searching for him before entering the service of Aphrodite. This led to Psyche being reunited with Eros.

Deucalion and his wife Pyrrha fared better than most mortals. He was the son of Prometheus and she the daughter of Pandora, and together they ruled a kingdom in northern Greece during the third, or Bronze, Age. The people of the preceding Golden and Silver Ages were wise and virtuous, but those of the Bronze Age were violent and brutish, and did not honour the gods properly. Zeus decided to destroy humanity with a great flood, but Deucalion and Pyrrha were warned and sailed to safety in a chest. Some sources say they were the only survivors but others mention people – including whole tribes – who found a way to escape destruction. On the instructions of the oracle at Delphi, Deucalion and Pyrrha created a new race of men and women out of rocks.

ABOVE: Zeus took on many forms in order to mate with human women, possibly because anyone seeing his true form would be destroyed like Semele, daughter of the hero Cadmus. He seduced Leda in the form of a swan.

THE LEGACY OF GREEK MYTHOLOGY

The Ancient Greeks created the foundations of modern literature, art and science, and their mythology has influenced subsequent cultures to the present day. Some stories are so well known that they have given us names for concepts the Ancient Greeks could never have imagined.

An apparently harmless or even useful piece of computer code that turns out to be a deceptive method of getting past defences was dubbed a Trojan after the Trojan horse; an organism containing genetically different tissues is called a Chimera. Other influences are less direct than the use of names but are powerful all the same.

The Legacy of Troy

After Homer and Hesiod wrote their epic tales in the first years after the Greek Dark Age, many others embellished and added to their work. Some of them simply retold the stories or added

OPPOSITE: **In Virgil's** *Aeneid,* **Latinus was the king of Latium who welcomed Aeneas to his court. Aeneas' marriage to Latinus' daughter Lavinia was one of the steps that led to the foundation of Rome.**

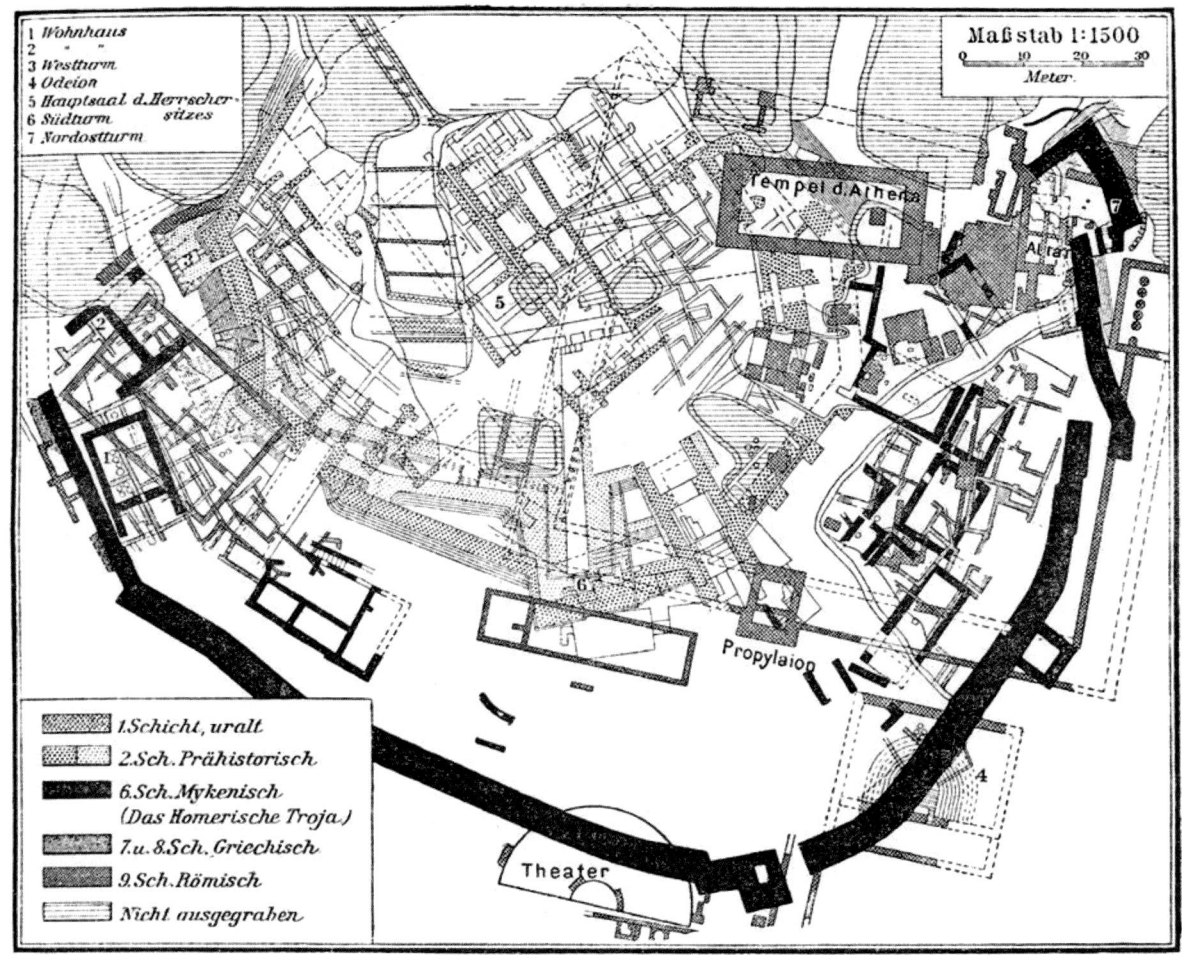

ABOVE: Heinrich Schliemann's excavations proved that there was indeed a city on the site of Troy, and that it had suffered in war. It is possible that the *Iliad* was derived from oral histories of that conflict, though by no means certain.

extra myths to an existing framework, but others went far beyond the existing texts. Among them were philosophers like Plato, who used concepts from Greek mythology to make philosophical points that had nothing to do with religion. Plato's tale of orderly and right-thinking Athens freeing the world from the tyranny of degenerate and undisciplined Atlantis was no religious tale; it was a philosophical metaphor.

The *Iliad*, *Odyssey* and works like them were considered to be histories by many, and it is possible that in some places they were historically accurate. In the 1870s, Heinrich Schliemann instigated an archaeological investigation into a suspected site of Troy. His work uncovered successive cities dating back to the Bronze Age, with fortifications that may have first been constructed 5000 years ago.

This does not, of course, prove that Athena rode in Diomedes' chariot or that Ares was wounded on that very spot, but it does suggest that events described in ancient texts might have had a basis in reality. The line between mythology, history and pure invention was crossed and recrossed many times by writers using the stories of the Trojan Wars as a basis.

Virgil

The Roman epic poet Virgil wrote his *Aeneid*, the story of Aeneas, around 30–20BC. In it he told of Aeneas' wanderings around the Mediterranean, his time at the court of Queen Dido of Carthage, and his settling in Italy, which led to the founding of Rome. Many of the popular myths surrounding the settlement of that city revolve around Trojans fleeing the destruction of their home.

Virgil used Homer's work and his poetic style as a basis for his own tale, and others followed much later. The *Historia Brittonum*, published around AD829 and for several centuries considered to be factual, claims that a descendant of Aeneas, named Brutus, settled in Britain and gave the country its name. The concept was expanded by Geoffrey of Monmouth when he published his *Historia Regum Britanniae* in the early 1100s.

LEFT: The story of Aeneas and Dido, Queen of Carthage, was expanded in the late 1600s into an opera by Purcell. Its origins run through book IV of Virgil's *Aeneid* and back to Homer's work.

Geoffrey of Monmouth

According to Geoffrey of Monmouth, Brutus founded a city named Troy Nova, after which the local tribe was named. These were the Trinovantes and their city, its name corrupted to Trinovantum, eventually became London. The line of British kings descended from these first Trojan settlers included King Arthur.

Geoffrey of Monmouth's work barely coincides with actual history, of course, and even where it begins to touch upon known events it is highly inaccurate. However, the legacy of Troy can be traced through these works from the *Iliad* to the founding of Rome and the story of Arthur, King of the Britons.

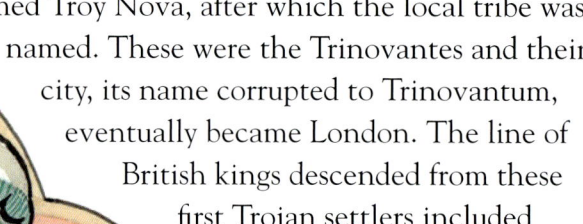

LEFT: Geoffrey of Monmouth first introduced the character who would become King Arthur in his *Historia Regum Brittaniae*.

NORSE GODS IN TROY

Others used mythical Troy as a component in their own works. Snorri Sturluson, an Icelandic Christian monk writing in around AD1200, recorded much of what we know about Norse mythology. He was writing long after Christianity had displaced the old Norse religion, and large parts of his work were highly distorted – not least because he had to avoid the disapproval of the Church. Sturluson records a tale where the Norse gods dwell in Troy and travel to Asgard each day over the rainbow bridge Bifrost.

More recent works, which usually make no attempt to pretend to be anything but fiction, use Troy as the origin point for objects or a setting for precursor events. It has become a convenient, well-known 'ancient place of power and mystery' recognized by readers and viewers without requiring much explanation. These works should perhaps give Homer a co-writing credit for establishing such a convenient backstory.

Cultural Influences

Herodotus is widely credited with being the 'father of history'. He used a method not previously seen, writing factually about places and events in a manner that is now very familiar. Although Herodotus was not recording myths and legends, there is a considerable amount of mythology within his writing because it was part of the popular culture of the day. Indeed, after his death in around 425 BC, his work was divided into nine books, each named after one of the Muses.

Others followed in Herodotus' footsteps, and arguably refined his style into a more rigorous historical methodology. Thucydides, writing around the same time, made use of eyewitness accounts and verifiable statements, whereas Herodotus has been accused of inserting hearsay and questionable statements to make his history more interesting.

Around 370 BC, Xenophon wrote *Anabasis*, a historical account of how a 10,000-strong force of Greek mercenaries marched out of Persia after being abandoned by their paymaster's faction. While these writers and others like them were creating what might be termed works of historical non-fiction, they helped ensure that Greek culture and the events surrounding Ancient Greece would be preserved and passed down. Their contribution to Western literature meant that the myths of their people would also continue to fascinate readers down the ages.

BELOW: Herodotus is widely credited as the 'father of history', though his work trod a line between reporting known and verifiable facts and relating wild tales which were not backed by any evidence.

The Olympic Games

The Olympic Games also serve to remind modern generations about Ancient Greek mythology. There are many stories surrounding the establishment of regular games at Olympia. Some say that Zeus commanded it after defeating Chronos on that spot; others that they were founded by Heracles in thanks for Zeus' assistance in overthrowing King Augeas. This was in revenge for Augeas' refusal to pay Heracles the agreed fee for cleaning out his stables and subsequently banishing him when he protested.

Another legend states that King Pelops competed against King Oenomaus in a chariot race. The prize was the right to marry Oenomaus' daughter Hippodamia, and losing challengers were to be put to death. Pelops cheated, loosening the wheel of his opponent's chariot, which caused him to be killed in the ensuing crash. This fulfilled a prophecy that Oenomaus would be killed by his son-in-law, which he had been trying to avert. This typically convoluted Greek tale states that Pelops ordered the games to be held every four years as a celebration.

ABOVE: **King Pelops is credited with founding the Olympic Games as a celebration of him winning a chariot race by cheating.**

Thus the legends of the Olympics are as bloodthirsty as most others. The great unifying games, a symbol of intense but friendly and peaceful competition, were founded after regicide, revolution or a battle between the gods. It was not uncommon in that time for athletes to be killed in the games – or to accidentally kill someone as they competed – so the Ancient Greeks would have thought nothing of this.

Roman Variations

Traditionally, the city of Rome is said to have been founded in 753BC, by the descendants of refugees from the sack of Troy. In the early years of the city, Greece was the dominant power in the Mediterranean, and it is unsurprising that the early Romans were heavily influenced by Greek culture. Over time, a Romanized version of the Greek myths appeared, with gods often given new Latinized names; Iris and Apollo are notable exceptions.

Eventually, Rome conquered the Mediterranean world, including Greece, and imposed its version of the Greco-Roman mythology on the wider world. The great literary tradition inherited from the Greeks ensured that there were many works of history and myth, and the size and prosperity of the empire meant that documents and monuments would survive.

One result of this co-opting of Greek culture was an overlay of additional myths and rationalizations that sometimes makes it difficult to discern the original story. Elements that did not appear until the writings of Ovid and Virgil are now intertwined with the stories of Homer and Hesiod. While some might be considered anachronisms, most of these additions sit well enough within the overall story – which may have been amended to accommodate them – that the result is an expanded and rationalized myth rather than an obvious distortion.

The close similarities between these two mythologies mean that it is very common to become confused about which gods are Roman and which are Greek. Some Roman versions of the Greek

BELOW: The Roman Bacchus, god of wine, was a rather more jolly and pleasant sort of person than his Greek equivalent. Dionysus was associated with madness and frenzy, drunken excess and other antisocial aspects of consuming wine.

gods seem to have endured nothing more than a rebranding exercise, but others were different to the originals in some ways. The Greek myths were filtered through the perception of a different culture after centuries of evolution, which inevitably imposed some changes. Thus the Roman Bacchus, ostensibly the equivalent of Dionysus, was a simpler and more jolly individual than the Greek god who brought madness and frenzy along with wine.

Dante's *Inferno*

Virgil, Ovid and other Roman writers produced works that drew on the original Greek versions or were sequels to them, and these in turn influenced later writers. In some cases the writers themselves became characters in later works. Virgil appears in Dante's *Inferno* as a guide through the nine layers of hell, which contain a number of familiar elements and characters.

In the *Inferno*, the first layer of hell was in fact a rather poor version of heaven, the destination for decent-but-non-Christian souls. Several figures from Greek history were present, notably Homer. In the second layer of hell, reserved for those who committed the sin of lust, Dante encountered Helen of Troy. This is perhaps a little unfair; she was seduced by Paris using the power of Aphrodite. However, given how merciless the Greek

RIGHT: Aeneas and his son Ascanius are credited with founding Rome, though as usual there are several versions of the tale. In some, Ascanius is the daughter of Aeneas and Lavinia, daughter of King Latinus.

gods tended to be, eternal punishment for falling victim to their machinations is not out of character.

The river Styx lay in the fifth circle of hell, where those who committed the sin of wrath were punished, and Dante encountered centaurs in the seventh circle. The centaurs of Greek myth were notoriously brutal, so a place in the realm reserved for the most violent sinners may have been merited. Part of the ninth, and nastiest, circle of hell was named for Antenora, an advisor to Priam of Troy.

Dante's use of elements of Greek mythology in his work was one of many elements contributing to confusion over what belongs in which mythology. Dante referred to his first circle of hell as Limbo. There are parallels to Ancient Greek tales of souls who could not pay the ferryman to take them across the Styx and were forced to linger, but Dante's limbo is a final destination rather than a place to become stuck on the way to one.

Religious Parallels

Ancient Greece and Egypt had a great deal of contact and influenced one another. There are shared elements between the two, such as the existence of the Sphinx in both cultures, and many more parallels between ostensibly different religions. The same applies to Persian religions, whose gods were in many cases co-opted into Greek mythology.

Greek and Norse parallels

Parallels are even more apparent between the Greek and Norse religions. It is possible that there were direct influences; many Norsemen served as mercenaries in the Byzantine Empire, and others raided or traded widely. Some Germanic and Norse stories mention Greek and Eastern European figures. Many of the gods are at least similar, though that may be due to the nature of mythology rather than direct influence. Thunder-gods, warriors and goddesses of love or fertility are common to many religions, and could arise out of the mythological need for one or be extrapolated from human experience.

The cosmology of Greek and Norse religions is broadly similar; a world formed from a void containing all potential is

OPPOSITE: **The wars of the Norse gods against their predecessors, the Jotnar or giants, bore many similarities with Greek mythology. In both, a thunderbolt-hurling god led the fight, though Thor was not the leader of the Norse gods.**

not very different from one that sprang from an abyss where fire and ice met and became the stuff of the universe. Both had an underworld where the dead were, and plenty of monsters for their gods to battle. The most striking similarity is the overthrow of the previous gods.

Where Zeus and his followers were the children of the Titans and ultimately cast them down, Odin and the Norse gods were the children of the Jotnar, or giants. However, while Zeus and the Olympians seem to have won a permanent victory over their enemies, the Norse gods could expect a final battle when the Jotnar returned. Thus there are parallels and also differences, and it is difficult to say for certain whether any elements were directly co-opted. Some degree of influence is, however, possible.

Greek and Christian parallels

Similarly, there was considerable crossover between early Christian writings and the Greek myths. The Eastern Roman Empire, and later the Byzantine Empire that followed it, included Greece and the surrounding lands, and contained many peoples descended from Greeks. The new religion did not instantly sweep away the old; folk tales were still told and in some places the old gods were worshipped long after official conversion to Christianity had taken place.

As a result, early Christianity was heavily influenced by traditional Greek beliefs. While the old gods were discredited, some aspects of worship were retained and elements of their character or powers seeped into Christian works. The vengeful, smite-happy god of the Old Testament seems oddly reminiscent of Zeus and at times seemed equally willing to inflict savage punishment on mortals for apparently minor transgressions.

Oracles, Astrology and Astronomy

The Ancient Greeks gave us the modern constellations and stories of how they came to be. The position of planets in relation to these constellations was thought to be significant in ancient times, a tradition that has passed down to modern times as astrology. The idea that events can be to some extent predicted by the position of stars and planets is strengthened by

210 THE LEGACY OF GREEK MYTHOLOGY

a belief in fate or some kind of cosmic order. The Ancient Greeks believed that the Moirae determined a person's fate at the time of his or her birth; it follows that if a person's fate was fixed then it could be read by those who knew how.

The Greeks encountered astrology, in the form of an organized body of knowledge, due to interactions with other cultures to their east. Around 200BC, Greek scholars began writing detailed works that described a recognizable zodiac. Ptolemy, writing around AD150, laid the foundations of modern astrology. His system of planets, transits and houses has been used with little change ever since.

Ptolemy also postulated a geocentric view of the cosmos, with a flat earth at the centre. What became known as the Ptolemaic System provided an accurate model for the movements of the

BELOW: The Ptolemaic system of constellations and houses has been in use for nearly 2000 years, with little change. The Ancient Greeks observed the same stars we do, and may have interpreted similar meanings from their positions.

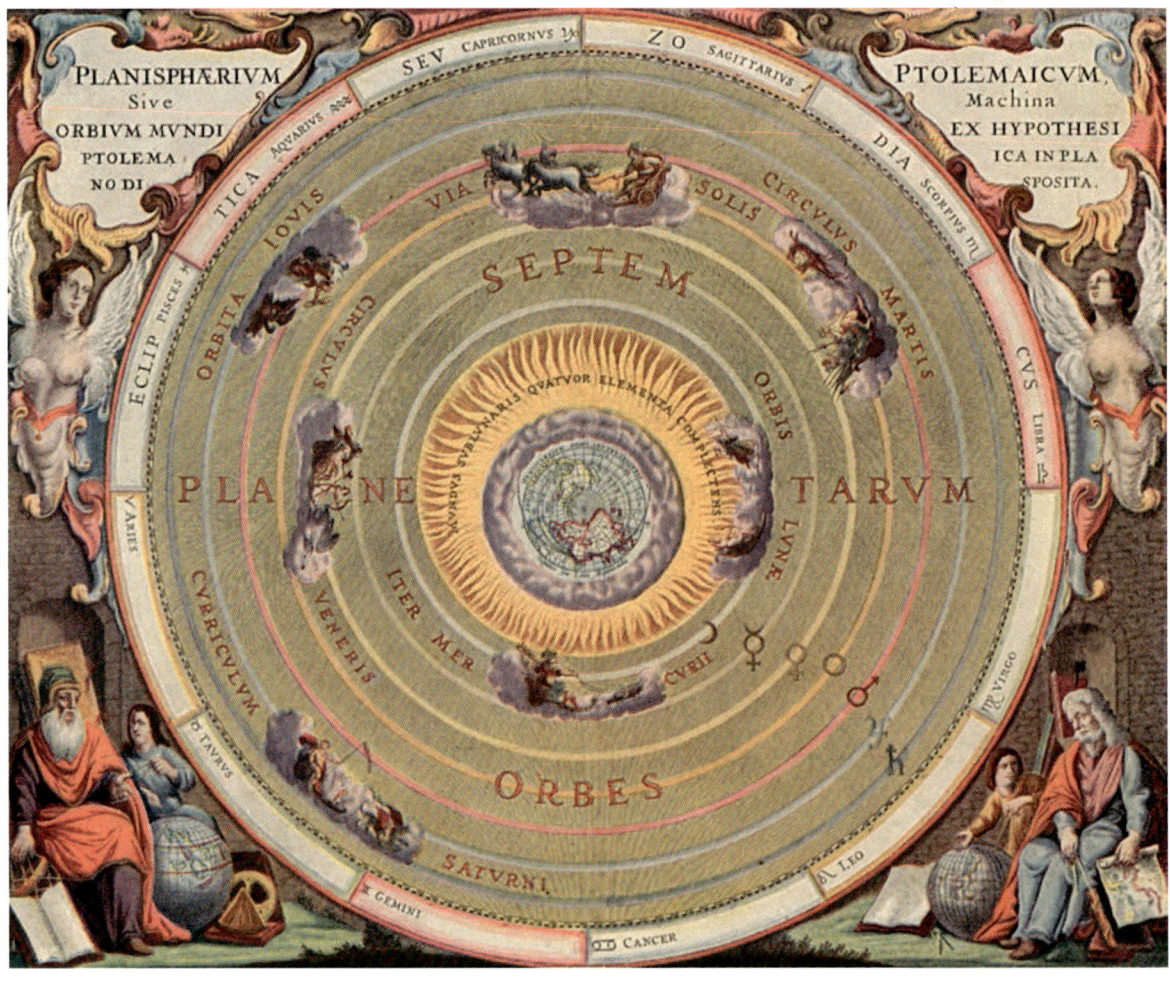

planets and was accepted for centuries. It used the same concept of nested spheres with planets and stars fixed to them as previous Greek models.

In this era, astronomy and astrology were essentially the same thing, and much early scientific work was done using the same observations of heavenly movement as astrologers would look for. Over time, the two diverged, but even today Greek legends play an important part in space exploration.

Although the planets of our solar system are named for Roman gods, many other bodies are given names from Greek mythology. The first four moons of Jupiter to be discovered were named Ganymede, Callisto, Io and Europa – all characters associated with Zeus. Tethys, Dione, Rhea and Iapetus, moons of Saturn, were all Titans, and the largest moon in the solar system is named Titan.

Greek legend provides an all-but-endless source of designations for newly discovered moons and bodies, and also names for space missions and probes. The Helios probes were sent to study the sun's processes; early manned missions were named Gemini and Mercury – the Roman equivalent of Hermes. The moon landing missions, arguably the most audacious endeavour in human history, were named for Apollo, the god of light and knowledge. While it is unlikely that NASA hoped for divine patronage, the association of these missions with mythological figures and their big stories was appropriate – a grand endeavour needs a suitably auspicious title.

Greek Myth in Literature and Art

Greek mythology has proven a rich source for work in other genres. Shakespeare used a great deal of Greco-Roman imagery in some of his plays, and some characters are recognizable as being based on mythological equivalents. Likewise, a number of operas have been written about the characters of Greek myth. Notable among them is Dido and Aeneas, which is based on the work of Virgil, who in turn drew on Homer's *Iliad*.

The opera tells how Aeneas was happy at Carthage with its queen Dido, but was tricked into believing he was being ordered to leave her by the gods. His instructions were to go to Italy to

ABOVE: Ourania, whose name means heavenly was the Muse of astronomy. Observations of the stars were vitally important to navigation, agriculture and the correct timing of sacrifices.

BELOW: More commonly known as the Venus de Milo, the Aphrodite of Milos is thought to have been carved around 100BC. It is perhaps the best-known of Ancient Greek sculptures, and is on display at the Louvre in Paris.

found a city there, although his enemies intended that he would perish at sea. Dido learned of his intention to leave. Although Aeneas told her he would stay after all, she chose instead to send him away and die of a broken heart.

Another example is *Orpheus in the Underworld*, which told the story of the great musician and sometime Argonaut, Orpheus as he journeyed into the realm of Hades to win back his dead wife Eurydice. The opera put a satirical slant on the rather dour subject matter, and also lampooned other operas with a more serious tone. As with many such works, *Orpheus in the Underworld* used Roman names for the gods, which were in turn derived from the Greek.

Artists have for centuries depicted notable figures and events from Greek mythology in statues, paintings and mosaics. Painted vases and mosaics were created during the Ancient Greek era that survive to this day. It is sometimes difficult to determine which gods are depicted in any given case, especially when a god had more than one aspect or similar deities existed, but these images are invaluable in preserving what the Ancient Greeks considered their gods to look like.

Later artists sometimes remained faithful to the original images, and sometimes indulged in what might today be described as reimagining the gods and heroes. These images

JAMES JOYCE'S *ULYSSES*

Dido and Aeneas took part of a larger tale, itself derived from a relatively minor character in the *Iliad*, and expanded it into a complete story. This approach has been used by other writers and musicians, though some instead took stylistic inspiration from the epic poems of Ancient Greece. Among them was James Joyce, whose novel *Ulysses* takes place over the course of one day in the life of a fairly ordinary man in twentieth-century Dublin.

Structurally, the novel *Ulysses* was based upon the *Odyssey* – Ulysses was the Roman name for Odysseus – and each chapter echoes a particular segment of the original poem. Although the modern-day Ulysses lived a rather more mundane life than ancient Odysseus, the novel presents his journey through that one day in parallel to the great epic.

in turn influenced later art, making it possible to see how later societies visualized the mythological characters of Ancient Greece. It is possible to trace trends in changing social norms through the way a particular god was depicted. For example, Aphrodite – or Venus, as the Romans called her – always has to be supremely beautiful and desirable, since that is her core identity as a god, but exactly what that meant to any given generation is revealed through their depictions of her.

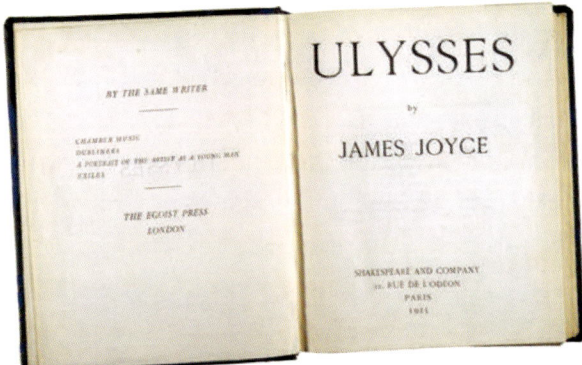

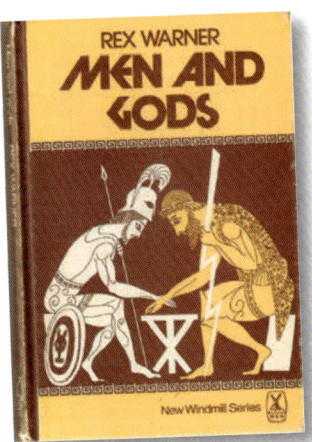

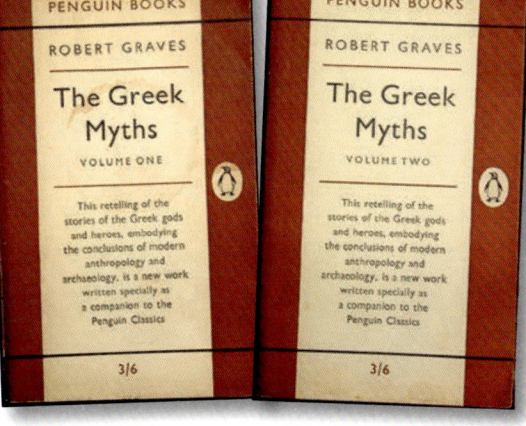

LEFT: The stories of Conan the Barbarian drew on elements of Greek myth and also the heroic-adventurer style of literature pioneered by Homer's *Iliad* and *Odyssey*. With these tales, Robert E. Howard and his successors popularized the modern sword-and-sorcery genre.

Echoes of Homer and Hesiod

The tales of Heracles, Jason and other Greek heroes were the archetypes for tales of heroic adventurers that followed. The format was generally the same: an exceptional individual needed to complete some task to obtain an object – a 'plot token' as it is sometimes called – or outcome. This might be absolution for a crime, permission to marry someone's daughter or the return of their inheritance.

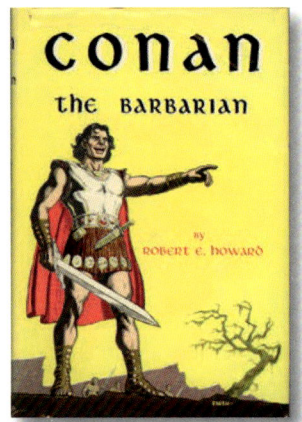
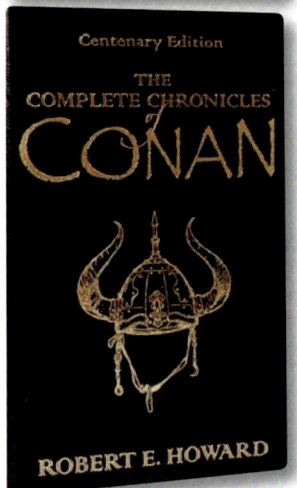
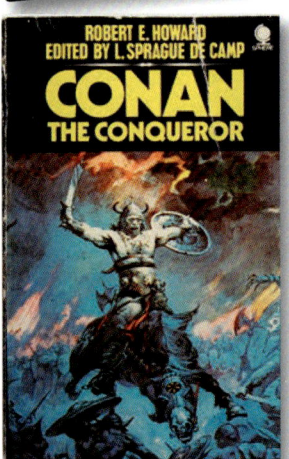

ABOVE: Conan the Barbarian has appeared in magazines, books, comics and several films.

Perhaps the archetypical heroic adventurer of modern literature was Robert E. Howard's Conan the Barbarian. Conan was not supernatural in origin and had little interaction with his gods other than a couple of interventions by Crom, but he did exist in a world where gods and supernatural creatures stalked the earth. This was Hyboria, a supercontinent that existed after 'the years when the oceans drank Atlantis', and contained many recognizable elements of real-world mythologies.

Howard and those who continued his work drew inspiration from the heroic adventures of Heracles and other Greek heroes, and in places may have borrowed plot elements wholesale. Conan made long voyages to mysterious islands, sought magical treasures in remote places and became entangled in the machinations of kings. Although parodied in recent years and sometimes dismissed as simplistic sword-and-sorcery fodder, Howard's tales are a fitting continuation of the Homeric tradition; they are big stories with a big hero and a satisfying degree of both violence and wonder.

Some heroic stories are simple retellings of the Greek myths, or thinly veiled derivatives. Others have similarities that may be nothing more than coincidence. After all, there are only so many stories to tell and so many gods to write about. A learned warrior-god will inevitably be compared to Athena or Apollo; a swift messenger is likely to be compared to Hermes.

Sometimes there is more than one set of parallels to be found, which suggests that influences are present even if the overall

Greek mythology in rock music

Some uses of Greek mythology are both directly derivative and highly inventive. The Canadian rock band Rush told a tale on one of their albums of a space explorer who fell into the black hole of Cygnus X-1. On the next album, the song 'Hemispheres' tells of a war between the gods of love and reason, each group seeking to control the fate of humanity. Into this conflict came the disembodied spirit of the space traveller. He showed the gods that both emotion and reason were needed, and took his place among them as Cygnus, the god of balance.

storyline does not closely match one of the Greek epics. Both the original and rebooted versions of *Battlestar Galactica* feature refugees fleeing the destruction of their home and making a long voyage – an odyssey, as the saying goes – in search of a new one. Even characters' names are drawn from mythology, and in the rebooted series there are elements of Ancient Greek religion as well.

The reasons why authors, musicians or show creators use these elements can vary, but the usual one is that they are readily recognizable and give a cultural flavour to their setting that does not need much explanation. Sometimes the influence may be unintentional; the themes and style of Homer's tales are so intertwined in our culture that we can sometimes fail to notice them.

There are many examples in modern literature and entertainment, including movies that tell a story from Greek mythology or borrow from it to create a new tale about modern-day descendants of the Greek gods. Other works echo elements

BELOW: Relatively little is known of Homer. He is generally assumed to be a real person, perhaps a professional reciter of oral traditions, but there are those who believe that Homer's works were in fact produced by more than one author.

of the ancient myths without explicitly following them, such as the *Hunger Games* series, which has young people offered as competitors in a cruel deathmatch, the prize being adequate food for their home region.

A Mythical Bestiary and Lexicon

Part of the legacy of the Greek myths is the modern 'fantasy bestiary' used by many games and movies. Fantasy worlds that have virtually nothing to do with Ancient Greece often feature creatures from its mythology. Thus there are centaurs and tree spirits to be found in the remote woodlands, and the occasional minotaur or harpy to endanger adventurers.

The inclusion of these creatures in popular games has ensured a new lease of life for the Greek myths, although often a creature or monster appearing in a video game may be known by its fans for the powers and identity it has in the game rather than in the original mythology. All the same, the occasional argument about whether centaurs count as cavalry and where their vital organs are located can be interesting.

Such discussions may have been held in ancient times – the Greeks had a scientific mindset and might have wondered if a centaur would be disabled by an arrow in its human chest. Heracles evaded this question by using the blood of the Hydra as a poison, but a normal archer might be in for an unpleasant suppose after seeing his arrow apparently strike true.

Similarly, some of the magical treasures that appear in the Greek myths have parallels elsewhere, but the Greek version is the earliest known example. Garments – in the Greek case it

RIGHT: The centaur is one of what might be called 'standard fantasy creatures' encountered in modern fiction. According to this interpretation at least, a centaur can be killed by an arrow to its human torso.

was a cap or helmet owned by Hades – that could make the wearer invisible, magic shields and spears, and winged footwear all appear in modern and traditional adventure stories.

Greek mythology gave us this lexicon of magical components from which to build new tales of adventure, and it also showed what could be done. If a hero can borrow a god's chariot and fly across the skies, what limits really exist? It is this, more than anything else, that is the legacy of the Greek myths. They are a key to imagination and a showcase of how to build an exciting tale with mythic elements.

An Enduring Legacy

Homer and Hesiod are credited with producing the earliest works of Western literature, and their influence cannot be overestimated. The myths of the Ancient Greeks have passed into our modern culture to the point where they are ours as well as theirs. When explorers find a sunken city, it is hailed as 'the real Atlantis' and everyone knows what that means. A complex argument can be described as labyrinthine, and nobody wants to let a Trojan inside their firewall.

New characters with the names of ancient gods and heroes have appeared, creating a link all the way back to Homer. Some are fictional; some are real but very different from the original. Napoleon Bonaparte made his final surrender aboard the British warship *Bellerophon*, ending the Napoleonic Wars. At the beginning of World War II, the Allied light cruisers *Ajax* and *Achilles* – along with the heavier but more mundanely named *Exeter* – defeated the greatly superior pocket battleship *Graf Spee* at the Battle of the River Plate.

The names of Ancient Greek gods continue to echo in our modern consciousness. Apollo put men on the moon and Nike, we are told, brings victory in sport where she once was the arbiter of battle. These mythological figures are now as much a part of our cultural identity as they were in Ancient Greece. While their names live on, so too will their legends.

ABOVE: Hesiod's work, produced around 700BC, probably drew on legends from before the Greek Dark Age and it continues to be influential today.

BIBLIOGRAPHY

Buxton, Richard. *The Complete World of Greek Mythology*. London: Thames & Hudson, 2004

Evslin, Bernard. *Heroes, Gods and Monsters of the Greek Myths*. New York: Laurel Leaf Books, reprint 2001

Graves, Robert. *The Greek Myths: A Complete and Definitive Edition*. London: Penguin, reprint 2011

Hamilton. *Mythology: Timeless Tales of Gods and Heroes*. New York: Black Dog & Leventhal Publishers, 1942

Hesiod. *Hesiod and Theognis*. London: Penguin, reprint 2000.

Homer. *The Iliad*. London: Penguin, 1987.

Homer. *The Odyssey*. London: Penguin, reprint 2003

Herodotus. *The Histories*. London: Penguin, 1954

Kershaw, Steve. *The search for Atlantis: A History of Plato's Ideal State*. New York: Pegasus Books, 2018.

Ovid, *Metamorphoses*. Translated by David Raeburn. London: Penguin, 2004

Plato, *The Complete Works*. USA: Hackett Publishing Co, 1997

Virgil. *The Aeneid*. London: Penguin, 2003.

INDEX

References to illustrations are in *italics*

Acastus, King 111, 112, 176
Acheron (River/God) 37, 104
Achilles 77, 112, 183–4, *186*, 186–7, 189
Acrisius, King 158, *158*, 161
Admetus, King 78
Adonis 76, 83, *83*
Aeetes, King 174–6, *174–5*
Aegeus, King 139, 177–80
Aegis 86
Aeneas 185, 198, 201, *201*, 206, 211–12
Aeneid (Virgil) 198, 201
Aeolus 104, 190
Aeson 170, 176
Aether 24, 26, 27
Aethra 178, 192
Africa 129, 145, 146
afterlife 72–5
  see also Elysium; Hades; Tartarus
Agamemnon, King 73–4, 77, 80, 182–4, 186, 187
Age of Heroes 51
Aigaion 38
Aigaios 100
Aigipan 151
Ajax 74, 186, 187
Alcestis 78
Alcmene 162–3, *163*
Alcyoneus 62–3, *63*
Alexander the Great 19, 20
Aloadai 124–5
Alpheius 108
Amazons 84, 131, *131*, 167–8, *167*, 180, 194
Amphitrite 66, *66–7*, 100, *101*, 109
Amykos, King 172
Anabasis (Xenophon) 203
Ananke 27, *73*, 73
Androgeus 139

Andromeda 151, 160–1, *160–1*
Anemoi 104, 105
animals, creation of 49
Antaeus 64
Antigone 110–11
Aphrodite 75–6, 77, 82–6, 86, 89, 181–2, *183*, 184, 185, 197
Apollo 21, 48, 77–8, *81*, 89, 117, 124, 169, *195*
  and Artemis 43, 77–82
  and Hermes 87–8, *88*
  musical contest with Pan 78, 115
  Trojan War 185, *185*, 186–7
Aquarius 151
Arachne 194
Archaic period 16–17
Ares 60, 76, 77, 82–5, *83*, *84*, 125, 137, 162, 185
Arethusa 108
Argo 171, *171*, 177
Argonauts 171–7
Argus Panoptes 89, *123*, 125
Ariadne 117, 118, 179–80, *179*
Aries 149
Arimaspoi 144, *145*
Aristaios 99
Aristotle 24
art (mythology in) 212–13
Artemis 77, *79*, 89, 94, *94*, 108, 125, 144, 164, 183, *195*
  and Apollo 43, 77–82
  boar 141–2
Asclepius 81, *116*, 117
Asteria 43, 45
Astraia 150–1
Astraios 45
astrology 208–11
astronomy 24, 30, 74, 149–52, 208–11
Astydameia 111–12
Atalanta *141*, 142, 171
Athamas, King 88, 90, 103
Athena 62, 84–6, *126*, 146, 192

  and Arachne 194
  and Athens 65
  birth of 58, 85
  and Cadmus 162
  and Gigantomachy 63, 64
  and Jason and the Argonauts 171
  life of 85–6
  and Medusa 68, 161
  and Paris of Troy 86, *86*, 181–2, *183*
  and Perseus 158–9, 161
  Trojan War 184, 185, 187
Athens 17–19, 65, 85, 139, 154, 179–80
Atlantis 31, 152–5, *153*, *155*
Atlas 45, 105, *105*, 160, 168
Atropos 98
Attis 99
Augeas, King 166, 204
Aurae 114
Auseans 146

Bacchus 205
Battlestar Galactica 215
Bellerophon 137, 192–4, *193*
Benthesikyme 66, 100, 105
Bia 46, 119
Blemmai 146
Boreas 104, 105, 144
Briareos 36, 38, 57, 100
Brutus 201, 202

Cadmus 161–2
Callisto *79*, 80, 151
Calydonian Boar 111, 141, 171, 178
Campe 143–4
Cancer 150
Capricorn 151
Cassandra 81, 187
Caucasian Eagle 144, 166
centaurs 40, *126*, 130–1, *130*, 151, 164–5, 207, 216, *216*

Cepheus, King 160
Ceryneian Hind *143*, 144, 164
Chaos 25–7, 29
Charites 59, 121–2
Charon 37
Chimera 136, *136*, *193*, 194
Chione 89, *89*, 105
Christianity 208
Chronos 28, 39, 39–42, 43, 46–7, 54, 55, 57
Chrysaor 68, 137, 160
Chryseis 183–4
Cinyras, King 78, 83
Circe 190–1, *192*
Classical era 17–19
Clotho 97–8
Clymene 44–5
Clytemnestra 182
Cocytus, River 37
Coeus 43
Conan the Barbarian 214
constellations 149–52, 208, 210–11
Corinth, Battle of (146BC) 20, *20*
Coronis 81, 117, 130
cosmos *see* universe
creation 25–9
Cretan Bull 139, 150, 167, 179, 196
Critias 152, 154
Crommyonian Sow 141, 178
cultural influences (of Greek mythology) 203–4, 211–17
Cyclopes 27, 36, 47, 48, 55, 65, 77, 132–3, *132*, 144, 190
Cyzicus, King 172

Daedalus 139, 196
daemons 49, 93
Danae 158, *158*
Dante 206–7
Daphne *81*, 82
dark age 14–15
death 72–5
Deianira 169
Demeter 66, 71, 87, *87*, 99, 116

democracy 18–19
Demophoon 87
Deucalion 50–1, *50*, 197
Dictys 158
Dido 201, *201*
Dido and Aeneas (opera) 211–12
Diomedes 85, 184–7, *185*
Diomedes, King 140, 167
Dionysus 53, 61–2, 64, 77, 88, 90–1, *91*, 103, *103*, 114, 118, 138
Doliones 172
Draco's code 16
Dryads 112

Echidna 134, 137
Echo 98–9, 115, *115*
Egypt 129
Elysium 36, 37, 72, 74
Endymion 43, 60–*1*, 61
Eos 41, 42–3, *42*, 45, 62, 104, 105, 114
Ephilates 124–5
Epicurus 24
Epigoni 184–5
Epimetheus 45, 49–50
Er 72–4, *73*
Eratosthenes *32*–3
Erebus 25, 26
Erginus, King 163–4
Eridanos, River 144, 145, 151
Erinyes 39, 95, *95*
Eris 85–6, 112, 121, 181
Eros 25, 27, 29, 76, 77, 82, 197
Erymanthean Boar 164, *166*
Eumolpus 105
Europa 161, *162*
Eurydice 112, *113*
Eurynome 39, 41, 59, 76, 108
Eurystheus, King 144, 164, 166–7, 169
Eurytion, King 110, 142
Eusebia 74–5
exploration 30–4, 148

fantasy bestiary 216–17

Fates 26, 64, 74, 97–8, *97*

Gaea 25, *25*, 26, 27, 36, 38–9, 40, 41, 55, 57, 62, 78
Galatea 103
Ganymede 119, 120, *120*, 144, 151
Gemini 150, *150*
Geoffrey of Monmouth 201, 202, *202*
geography 30–1, 32–5, 128–30
Geryon 134, 137, 168
giants 122–5
Gigantes 39, 55–7, 62–4
Gigantomachy 55–7, *55*, 62–4, 76
girdle of Hippolyta 167–8, *167*
Glaucus 102, 185
Golden Fleece 149, *149*, 170–1, 172, 175–6
Gorgades 147
Gorgons 103, 136–7, 158–60, *159*, 161
Graeae 103, 158
Greek peoples, origins of 8–11

Hades (God/place) 35–7, 43, 47, 48, 53, 68–9, *69*–72, 75, 112, 134, 169, 180–1
Harmonia 77, 82, 162
Harpyai 137, *137*, 172, *173*
Hebe 60, 119, *119*, 169
Hecate 43, 45, *45*, 71, 114, 116
Hecatoncheires 27, 36, 39, 47, 55, 57, 100, 143–4
Hector 185–7, 189
Hekaterides 100
Helen of Troy 86, 182, *182*, 184, 188–9, 206
Helios 41–2, 62, 67, 71, 97, 104, *104*, 168, 191
Helladic era 11–14
Hellenistic era 19–20
Hemera 26, 27, 42
Hephaestus 53, 58, 60, 64, *75*, 76–7, 82, 85, 91
Hera 59, 123
and Dionysus 62, 64, 90–1, 103

INDEX 221

and Echo 115
and Gigantomachy 63
and Hephaestus 76–7
and Heracles 62, 162–3
and Jason 170
and Paris of Troy 86, 86, 181–2, 183
and Zeus 57, 59–62, 125
Heracles 137, 156
   and Gigantomachy 55, 57, 62–4, 64
   and Hebe 119
   and Hera 62, 162–3
   and the Hydra 138, 138, 143
   and Jason and the Argonauts 171, 172
   and Karkinos 143
   and Kheiron 99, 151
   labours of 139, 140, 143, 144, 164–9, 164–6, 168–9
   life of 162–9
   and Olympic Games 204
   and Orthus 135
   and Theseus 180–1
Hermes 61, 64, 76, 78, 87–90, 88, 125, 158, 161
Herodotus 203, 203
Hesiod 24, 25, 26, 35, 36, 50, 51, 58, 121, 217, 217
Hesperides 92, 105, 114, 134, 168, 168
Hestia 53, 91
Hippokampoi 102, 133, 133
Hippolyta 167–8, 167
Hippolytus 180, 180
Hippopodes 147
Historia Brittonum 201
Historia Regum Britanniae 201
Homer 36, 37, 104, 206, 215, 217
   Iliad 34–5, 157, 181, 183, 187
   mythical world view of 29, 29, 51
   Odyssey 188–92
   and Zeus 54
Horae 45, 59, 95–7, 96, 150
Howard, Robert E. 214

humans, creation of 49–51
Hunger Games 216
Hyacinthus 82, 104
Hydra 138, 138, 143, 164, 167
Hygeia 116, 117
Hylas 172
Hyperborea 130, 144–5
Hyperion 41
Hypnos 26, 37, 120

Iapetionides 44
Iapetus 44
Iasion 99, 150
Icarus 196
Idomeneus 187–8
Iliad (Homer) 34–5, 157, 181, 183, 187
Inferno (Dante) 206–7
Ino 90, 103
Io 89, 123, 125
Iobates, King 192, 194
Iphigenia 80, 183
Iris 105, 106, 107, 172
Iron Age 51

Jason and the Argonauts 149, 170–7, 173, 174–5
Joyce, James 212
Judgement of Paris 86, 183
Jupiter 105, 211

Karkinos 143, 150
Kastor 150, 150, 163, 171, 181, 196–7
Keltoi 129
Kerberos 72, 134, 169
Keres 120–1
Keto 103
Ketos 160, 160
Kharybdis 133–4, 176, 191
Kheiron 40, 99, 99, 112, 126, 131, 151, 164–6, 170
Khronos 27, 28, 42
Kouretes 40, 100
Kratos 46, 119

Krios 45
Krios Krysomallos 149

Labours of Heracles 164–9
Lachesis 97–8
Ladon 103, 134, 151, 168
Latinus 198
laws 16
Leda 196–7, 197
Lemnos 171–2
Lenae 114
Leo 150
Lethe, River 37, 73
Leto 43, 43, 61, 77–8, 77, 79, 123
Leukothea 103, 103
Libra 150, 151
literature, Greek influences on 211, 212–17
Lykaon, King 195
Lykourgos, King 91

Macedonia 19–20
Maenads 118
Makhlyes 146
Marsyas 78
Medea 175–7, 177, 178–9
Medusa 67–8, 76, 136–7, 136, 158–60, 159, 161
Meleager 142–3, 142
Melicartes 103
Menelaus, King 182, 184, 188–9
Menoetius 45
Metaneira, Queen 87
Metis 46, 57, 58, 85, 108
Midas, King 78, 90, 91, 115
Minoan civilization 11–13
Minos, King 139, 179, 196
Minotaur 118, 139, 139, 179
Minyans 171–2
Mnemosyne 45, 122
Moirae 45, 59, 64, 97–8, 97, 210
Morpheus 120, 121
mortal realm 30–1
mortals, creation of 49–51
Muses 45, 122, 122

music, Greek influence on 211–12, 214
Mycenaean civilization 13–14
Myrmidons 181, 183, 184, 186
Myth of Er 72–4, *73*

Naiades 108–9, *109*
Narcissus 115, *115*
Nelus 170
Nemean Lion 138, 150, 164, *164*, 178
Nemesis 116–17
Neolithic era 10–11
Nephele 130, 149
Nereids 100, 102, *102*, 109, 160
Nereus 27, 102
Nessus 169
Nike 45, 119
Niobe 79, 195
Norse mythology 202, 207–8, *209*
Nuloi 147
Nyctimus 195
nymphs 107–14, *107*
Nyx 26, *26*

Oceanids 108
Odysseus 68, 74, 184, 186, 187, 188–92, *191*, 212
Odyssey (Homer) 188–92, 212
Oedipus 140, *140*
Oeneus, King 141, 142
Oenomaus, King 204
Okeanos (River/God) 29, *29*, 30–1, *37*, *41*
Olympic Games 170, 204
Oneiroi 120, *121*
opera 211–12
Oracles 127–8
Orion 80, *80*, 151
Orpheus 112, *113*, 171, 176
Orpheus in the Underworld (opera) 212
Orthrus 134, *135*, 140, 168
Otus 124–5
Ourania *211*

Palaeolithic people 10
Palamedes 189
Pallas 45, 58
Pan 78, 89, 98–9, *98*, 115
Pandai 146
Pandarus 184
Pandora 45, 49, 50
Panes 99, 114
Panotioi *146*, 147
Paris of Troy 86, *86*, 181–2, *183*, 184
Pasiphae, Queen 139, 196
Patroclus 186, *186*
Pegasus 68, 137, 160, 192, *193*, 194
Peleus 77, 85–6, 110–12, 142, 181, 183
Pelias 78, 170–1, *170*, 176
Peloponnesian War (431–404BC) 17–18
Pelops 195, 204
Penelope 188–9, 190–2
Periphetes 178
Persephone 68–9, 70–1, *70*, 76, 83, 87, 104, 137, 181
Perseus 68, 144, 151, *151*, 158–61, *158–61*, 169
Phaedra 180, *180*
Phaethon 105, 145, *145*
Phaiakians 132–3
phalanx warfare 18–19, *20*
Phanes 27, *27*
Philip II 19–20
Philomena 84
Phineas/Phineus, King 137, 172, *173*
Phlegethon, River 37
Phoebe 43
Pholus 151, 164
Phorcys 103
Pillars of Hercules 30, *30*, 31
Pirithous 169, 181
Pisces 151
Pittheus, King 178
planets 24, 30, 74, 105, 208, 210–11

Plato 24, 31, 72, 74, 97, 152, 154–5, 200
Polydectes, King 158, 161
Polydeukes 150, *150*, 171, 172, 181, 196–7
Polyphemus 103, 132, 190
Pontus 26, 27, 45
Poseidon 65–7
 and Athens 85
 and Atlantis 152
 chariot 133, *133*
 and Cretan bull 139
 gift of trident 47, 48, 65
 life of 64–8
 wife and children 66, 68, 100–2, 105, 178
Potamoi 103–4, 108
Priapus 99
primordial gods 25–9
Prometheus 44, 45, 48, 49, 57, 119, 165–6, *165*
Proteus, King 192, 194
Psyche 197
Ptolemy 210–11, *210*
pygmies 147, *147*
Pyrrha 50–1, *50*, 197
Pythagoras 24
Pytheas 148, *148*

reincarnation 72–5
religious parallels 207–8
Rhea 39–40, 43, 103
Rhode 66–7, 100
Roman variations 204–6
Rome 20, 21, 204
Rush (rock band) 214
rustic gods 98–100
Sagittarius 151
Salamis, Battle of (480BC) 17
Satyrs 114, 118
Schliemann, Heinrich 200, *200*
Sciapods 147
science 23–5
Sciron 178
Scylla 133–4, 176, 191
Sea Peoples 14

Selene 41, 42–3, 61, 62, 104
Semele 62, 90, 138, 162
Seven Against Thebes 184–5
Shakespeare, William 211
Silenus 90, 91, 114, 118
Silver Age 50
Sirens 137, 176, 191
Sisyphus 196
Skorpios 150
Skyphios 65, 65
Snorri Sturluson 202
Sphinx 140, 140
Spire of Necessity 74
stars 24, 30, 74, 149–52, 208, 210–11, 210
Sternopthalmoi 146
Stymphalian Birds 137, 166, 167, 174
Styx (River/God) 37, 45, 118, 207
Symplegades 172, 174
Syrinx 98

Talos 176
Tantalos, King 195–6
Tartarus 25, 30–1, 35–6, 36, 38, 47, 73, 75, 123, 125, 143–4, 196
Taurus 150
Taygete 144
Telchines 65
Telemachus 189, 192
Telephassa 161–2
Tereus, King 84
Tethys 41, 41
Thanatos 26, 120
Thaumas 27, 105
Theia 41
Themis 45, 48, 49, 59
Theseus 68, 84, 118, 139, 139, 177, 177, 178–81, 179–80
Thespius, King 163–4
Thetis 52, 57, 60, 76, 176, 181, 187
  and Peleus 85–6, 109–12, 110–11
Thucydides 203

Thule 130, 148
Timaeus (Plato) 152
Tiresias 189
Titanomachy 47, 47
Titans
  birth of 36–8
  father turns against them 38–40
  first-generation 40–3
  overthrow of 46–7, 48
  second-generation 44–6
Tithonus 42
Tityos 122–3, 124
Triptolemos 99, 150
Triton 66, 100, 100, 102
Tritones 102
Trojan horse 187, 188
Trojan War 76, 85–6, 112, 181–8, 189
Troy 34–5, 34, 182, 187
  legacy of 199–202
  siege of 183–4
Troy Nova 202
Twelve Labours of Heracles 164–9
Tyche 116–17
Typhon 56, 57, 64, 76, 134, 151
Tyro 170

Ulysses (Joyce) 212
underworld 35–6, 37
  monsters and creatures of 134–8
  see also Hades; Tartarus
universe 23–30
  stars/planets 24, 30, 74, 105, 149–52, 208–11
Uranides 40
Uranus 26, 27, 36, 38–9, 40, 41
Ursa Major 151
Venus de Milo 212
Virgil 37, 201, 206
Virgo 150

winds 104
world, map of 32–3

Xenophon 203

Zelus 119
Zephyrus 82, 104
Zeus 40, 42, 43, 45, 52
  and Asclepius 117
  and Atlantis 154
  birth of 22, 40
  birth of Athena 58, 85
  and Callisto 79, 80
  challenges to supremacy of 125
  creation of animals and mortals 49–51
  and Dionysus 90
  flood 50–1, 197
  and Gigantomachy 55–7, 62, 63–4
  as King of the Gods 54, 54–7
  and Lykaon 195
  and the Olympians 47–9
  and overthrow of Titans 46–7, 55
  and Persephone 70–2
  retinue of 118–19
  and Thetis 52, 112
  Trojan War 68, 181, 186
  wives and children of 57–62
zodiac 149–52, 210–11

PICTURE CREDITS

Alamy: 8 (Kevin Wheal), 12 (Hercules Milas), 13 (Melvyn Longhurst), 15 (De Luan), 16 bottom (Interfoto), 19 (G L Archive), 20 (Lanmas), 21 (Image Broker), 22 (Active Museum), 25 (Interfoto), 26 & 27 (Art Collection 2), 32/33 (North Wind Picture Archive), 41 (Image Broker), 44 (Classicpaintings), 45 (PvE), 48 top (Science History Images), 49 & 50 (Art Collection 2), 52 (Picture Art Collection), 54 (Ian Dagnall), 56 (Granger Collection), 58 (Photo 12), 63 (Azoor Photo), 64 (Julian Money-Kyrle), 66/67 (Matt Ragen), 68/69 (NMUIM), 70 (Pictures Now), 72 (AGE Fotostck), 73 (Falkensteinfoto), 75 (Picture Art Collection), 76 (Bildwissedition), 77 (Interfoto), 83 (Art Collection), 84 (Historic Images), 87 (Adam Eastland), 88 (Granger Collection), 92 & 97 (Interfoto), 98 (Lebrecht), 99 (Falkensteinfoto), 101 (Adam Eastland), 102 (BLM Collection), 103 (Old Images), 105 (Azoor Photo), 109 (History Collection), 110/111 (Active Museum), 115 (Superstock/Peter Barritt), 120 (Prisma Archivo), 126 (Pictures Now), 128/129 (Stefano Bianchetti), 130 (Artokoloro Quint & Lox), 131 (Lanmas), 136 top (Image Broker), 138 (Classicpaintings), 139 (Ivy Close Images), 141 (Science History Images), 142 (VPC Photo), 144 (Artokoloro Quint & Lox), 146 (Interfoto), 147 (Classic Image), 153 (Everett Collection), 156 (Universal Images Group), 158 (Ivy Close Images), 159 (North Wind Picture Archive), 161 & 164 (Prisma Archivo), 165 (Picture Art Collection), 166 (Jeff Morgan), 168 (Ian Dagnall Computing), 169 (Masterpics), 170 & 171 (Ivy Close Images), 173 (Granger Collection), 177 (Ivy Close Images), 179 (Painters), 180 (ART Collection), 182 (AGE Fotostock), 184 (Active Museum), 186 (Adam Eastland), 193 (The Artchives), 197 (Artexplorer), 200 (Oprea Nicolae), 201 & 204 (Artokoloro Quint & Lox), 205 (Art Reserve), 206 (Lanmas), 209 (Historic Images), 210 (Granger Collection), 211 (Prisma Archivo), 203 top right (Retrofoto), 217 (Roger Cracknell)

Alamy/Chronicle: 39, 80, 89, 95, 119, 132, 133, 137, 145, 148, 150, 155, 163, 185, 213 top left, 216

Alamy/Heritage Images: 10, 37, 65, 90, 106, 113, 121, 122, 124, 143, 149, 160, 183, 188, 189, 195, 202, 215

Alamy/Peter Horree: 11, 16 top, 17, 24, 60/61, 79, 86, 91, 94, 116, 123, 136 bottom, 140

Alamy/World History Archive: 28, 30, 31, 59, 81, 104, 107, 117, 191

Bridgeman Images: 36 (Look & Learn), 38 (Musee des Beaux Arts/Roger Viollet), 43 (Trustees of Watts Gallery), 96 (Bristol Museum & Art Gallery), 174/175 (The Henry Barber Trust, The Barber Institute of Fine Arts)

Dreamstime: 34 (GVictoria), 85 (Itechno), 203 (Sed Mak), 212 (Alexirina 27000)

Getty Images: 6 (Heritage Images), 9 (DEA/Dagli Orti), 29 (SPL/Sheila Terry), 40 (DEA/Dagli Orti), 42 (Print Collector), 47 (Heritage Images), 48 bottom (Universal Images Group/Phas), 55 (Mondadori Portfolio), 62 (Print Collector), 100 (DEA/Dagli Orti), 135 (Art Images), 151 & 167 (Print Collector), 198 (Heritage Images)

Shutterstock: 78 (PNIK)